PREPARING FOR THE SH

Workbook and Practice Questions from SHRM

2022 Edition

PREPARING FOR THE SHRM-CP® EXAM

WORKBOOK AND PRACTICE QUESTIONS FROM SHRM

2022 EDITION

Alexander Alonso, PhD, SHRM-SCP
Chief Knowledge Officer, SHRM
Nancy A. Woolever, MAIS, SHRM-SCP
Vice President, Certification, SHRM

SHRM creates better workplaces where employers and employees thrive together. As the voice of all things work, workers and the workplace, SHRM is the foremost expert, convener and thought leader on issues impacting today's evolving workplaces. With 300,000+ HR and business executive members in 165 countries, SHRM impacts the lives of more than 115 million workers and families globally. Learn more at SHRM.org and on Twitter @SHRM.

Library of Congress Cataloging-in-Publication Data
Names: Alonso, Alexander, editor. I Woolever, Nancy A., editor.
Title: Preparing for the SHRM-CP exam : workbook and practice questions from SHRM / Alexander Alonso and Nancy A. Woolever, editors.
Description: 2022 edition. I Alexandria, VA : SHRM, the Society for Human Resource Management, [2022] I Includes index.
Identifiers: LCCN 2022000793 (print) I LCCN 2022000794 (ebook) I ISBN 9781586445522 (paperback) I ISBN 9781586445577 (pdf) I ISBN 9781586445621 (epub) I ISBN 9781586445676 (mobi)
Subjects: LCSH: Personnel management--Examinations--Study guides. I Personnel management--Examinations, questions, etc. I Personnel departments--Employees--Certification.
Classification: LCC HF5549.15 .P77 2022 (print) I LCC HF5549.15 (ebook) I DDC 658.30076--dc23/eng/20220311
LC record available at https://lccn.loc.gov/2022000793
LC ebook record available at https://lccn.loc.gov/2022000794

Published in the United States of America   2022 EDITION

PB Printing   10 9 8 7 6 5 4 3 2 1

Contents

Acknowledgments

This workbook was made possible by the thoughtful and generous advice, guidance, and input of many smart and talented subject matter experts, especially the following:

Mark Smith, PhD, Director, HR Thought Leadership, SHRM

Selina Russ, Senior Specialist, Form Development, SHRM

Charles Glover, Manager, Exam Development & Accreditation, SHRM

Patricia Byrd, SHRM-SCP, Director, Certification Operations, SHRM

Scott Oppler, PhD, Senior Technical Advisor, Human Resource Research Organization (HumRRO)

Nicholas Schacht, SHRM-SCP, Chief Global Development Officer, SHRM

Jeanne Morris, Vice President, Education, SHRM

Susie Davis, Director, Digital Education, SHRM

Eddice L. Douglas, SHRM-CP, Senior Specialist, Educational Products, SHRM

We also gratefully acknowledge the scores of SHRM members, SHRM certificate holders, and exam candidates who provided input for this book.

Introduction

We applaud your decision to move your career in Human Resources forward by pursuing a certification with SHRM! To this end, this workbook is designed to help you prepare for the **SHRM Certified Professional (SHRM-CP)** exam.

Specifically, the SHRM-CP exam is designed to determine who has the level of competency and knowledge that is expected for HR professionals who perform (or will perform) operational work. This includes such duties as implementing policies, serving as the HR point of contact, and performing day-to-day HR functions.

On the other hand, the SHRM Senior Certified Professional (SHRM-SCP) designation is for HR professionals who are a bit more advanced in their careers. This level of professional primarily works in a strategic role, such as developing policies and strategies, overseeing the execution of integrated HR operations, directing the entire HR enterprise, and leading the alignment of HR strategies to organizational goal. Although the SHRM-CP and SHRM-SCP exams are very similar in structure, this workbook is focused exclusively on the SHRM-CP exam.

It is important to note that this workbook is designed to be used along with the official SHRM study guide: *Ace Your SHRM Certification Exam*. The study guide includes much additional information about the exam and exam preparation strategies, and it also includes a set of practice items from a combination of the SHRM-CP and SHRM-SCP exams.

In this SHRM-CP workbook, some of the key concepts that were introduced in the study guide are further explained. For example, a self-assessment for gauging strengths and development areas that are addressed in the exam was briefly introduced in the study guide; this is created in the current workbook to help with SHRM-CP exam preparation.

Perhaps most importantly, this workbook includes an additional set of forty practice test items that were used on past SHRM-CP exams. These practice items will provide you with more exposure to the types of items that you will see on the real exam, as well as feedback about correct/incorrect responses. Plus, information is included about the difficulty level of the items, which can help even more in determining your understanding of the areas covered on the SHRM-CP. And again, these items were not simply created for this book—they were taken from real SHRM-CP exams that were used in previous years.

SHRM-CP and SHRM-SCP Eligibility

SHRM Certified Professional (SHRM-CP)

- The SHRM-CP certification is for individuals who perform general HR/HR-related duties or for those pursuing a career in Human Resource Management.
- Candidates for the SHRM-CP certification are not required to hold an HR title and do not need a degree or previous HR experience to apply; however, a basic working knowledge of HR practices and principles is recommended.
- The SHRM-CP exam is designed to assess the competency level of those who engage in HR work at the operational level. Work at this level includes duties such as implementing HR policies, supporting day-to-day HR functions, or serving as an HR point of contact for staff and stakeholders.
- Refer to the SHRM BASK for detailed information on proficiency standards for this credential (i.e., Proficiency Indicators for All HR Professionals).

SHRM Senior Certified Professional (SHRM-SCP)

- The SHRM-SCP certification is for individuals who have a work history of at least three years performing strategic level HR/HR-related duties or for SHRM-CP credential holders who have held the credential for at least three years and are working in, or are in the process of transitioning to, a strategic level role.
- Candidates for the SHRM-SCP certification are not required to hold an HR title and do not need a degree to apply.
- The SHRM-SCP exam is designed to assess the competency level of those who engage in HR work at the strategic level. Work at this level includes duties such as developing HR policies and procedures, overseeing the execution of integrated HR operations, directing an entire HR enterprise, or leading the alignment of HR strategies to organizational goals.
- Applicants must be able to demonstrate that they devoted at least one thousand hours per calendar year (Jan.–Dec.) to strategic level HR/HR-related work. More than one thousand hours in a calendar year does not equate to more than one year of experience.
- Part-time work qualifies as long as the one-thousand-hour per calendar year standard is met.
- Experience may be either salaried or hourly.
- Individuals who are HR consultants may demonstrate qualifying experience through the HR/HR-related duties they perform for their clients. Contracted hours must meet the one-thousand-hour standard.
- Refer to the SHRM BASK for detailed information on proficiency standards for this credential (i.e., Proficiency Indicators for All HR Professionals and for Advanced HR Professionals).

How to Apply

SHRM offers both certification exams during two testing windows every year. The first window is from May 1 to July 15, and the second window is from December 1 to February 15. Examinees can choose to take the exam in person at one of more than 500 Prometric testing centers across more than 85 countries with up to 6,000 seats daily, or they can choose to take it via live remote proctor.

Once you have decided which exam to take, register to take the exam on the SHRM website anytime between the Applications Accepted Starting Date and the Standard Application Deadline. Examinees who apply by the Early-Bird Application Deadline and/or who are SHRM members receive a reduced exam fee. Note that exam applications apply for specific testing windows; once you have applied, transfers to the following testing windows are possible but involve a separate transfer fee.

To register, you will:

1. Create a user account.

2. Select which level exam you want to take.

3. Complete the application form and sign the SHRM Certification Candidate Agreement.

4. Pay the registration fee.

5. Once you receive your Authorization-to-Test (ATT) letter, schedule your exam. Your ATT letter will outline several ways to schedule.

ONLINE
Learn More about How to Apply for the Exam

https://www.shrm.org/certification/apply/Pages
/applicationprocess.aspx

Section 1

The SHRM-CP Exam Structure

Types of Exam Items

As defined in the SHRM study guide and on the SHRM website, there are two general types of items on the SHRM-CP exam: (1) knowledge items (KIs)/foundational knowledge items (FKIs) and (2) situational judgment items (SJIs).

Knowledge items (including FKIs) are stand-alone multiple-choice items with four response options. Each KI tests a single piece of knowledge or application of knowledge.

Situational judgment items (SJIs) present realistic situations from workplaces throughout the world. Based on the scenario presented, SJIs ask test takers to consider the problem presented in the question within the context of the situation, and then select the best course of action to take. As with the KIs, these are multiple-choice items with four response options.

Exam Items

The SHRM-CP exam consists a total of 134 questions. This exam is broken into two equal halves, and each half contains 67 questions. Each half is divided into three sections:

» **Section 1:** 20 KIs and FKIs (i.e., knowledge items for behavioral competencies)

» **Section 2:** 27 SJIs

» **Section 3:** 20 KIs and FKIs

Exam Timing

The total exam appointment time is four hours, which includes three hours and forty minutes of testing time for the exam itself.

The exam time is broken down into:

» **Introduction,** including confidentiality reminder: four minutes

» **Tutorial:** eight minutes

» **Exam Half 1:** up to one hour and fifty minutes

» **Exam Half 2:** up to one hour and fifty minutes

» **Survey:** six minutes

There are a few transition screens throughout the exam that account for the remaining minutes.

Section 2

The SHRM BASK

One of the most important things for you to understand as you prepare for the SHRM-CP exam is this:

All of the HR competencies and knowledge areas that are assessed on the SHRM-CP exam are detailed in the SHRM BASK.

You can find the complete version of the SHRM BASK at

https://www.shrm.org/certification/about/BodyofAppliedSkillsandKnowledge/Pages/Download-SHRM-BASK.aspx

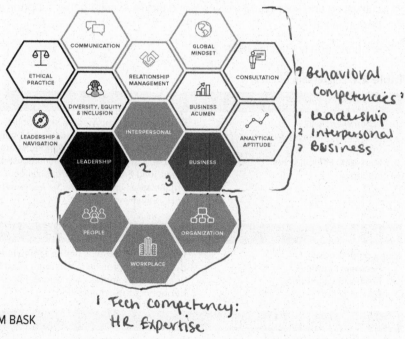

Figure 2.1. The SHRM BASK

Again, it is very important to remember that if something is not covered in the SHRM BASK, it is not eligible for the SHRM-CP exam. However, we should note that the SHRM BASK is an expansive document that covers many different areas, and you might not see everything in the BASK represented on the SHRM-CP exam in any given testing window.

Components of the SHRM BASK

Just to give you a sense of what is in the SHRM BASK (and therefore eligible for the SHRM-CP exam), we include definitions of the key components in each of the areas. For instance, the Leadership cluster is comprised of three separate competencies (each of which has a set of sub-competencies).

Leadership Cluster

Key components of Leadership behavioral competencies include the following:

» setting and implementing a vision and direction for the HR function

» managing or leading organizational initiatives

» influencing and supporting other organizational members and leaders

» driving an ethical organizational environment

» behaving in an ethical manner that promotes high standards of integrity and the organization's values

» cultivating and supporting a diverse and inclusive culture that supports organizational performance

» ensuring equity effectiveness

Table 2.1. Leadership Cluster

Leadership & Navigation	
Sub-competencies: » Navigating the organization » Vision » Managing HR initiatives » Influence	**Definition:** the knowledge, skills, abilities, and other characteristics (KSAOs) needed to create a compelling vision and mission for HR that aligns with the strategic direction and culture of the organization, accomplish HR and organizational goals, lead and promote organizational change, navigate the organization, and manage the implementation and execution of HR initiatives.
Ethical Practice	
Sub-competencies: » Personal integrity » Professional integrity » Ethical agent	**Definition:** the KSAOs needed to maintain high levels of personal and professional integrity and to act as an ethical agent who promotes core values, integrity, and accountability throughout the organization.
Diversity, Equity & Inclusion (DE&I)	
Sub-competencies: » Creating a diverse and inclusive culture » Ensuring equity effectiveness » Connecting DE&I to organizational performance	**Definition:** the KSAOs needed to create a work environment in which all individuals are treated fairly and respectfully, have equal access to opportunities and resources, feel a sense of belonging, and use their unique backgrounds and characteristics to contribute fully to the organization's success.

Interpersonal Cluster

Key components of Interpersonal behavioral competencies include the following:

» networking

» building and maintaining professional relationships and teams

» successfully managing conflict and negotiations

» clearly and effectively communicating with stakeholders

» operating within a global workforce

» advocating for a culturally diverse and inclusive workplace

Table 2.2. Interpersonal Cluster

Relationship Management	
Sub-competencies: » Networking » Relationship building » Teamwork » Negotiation » Conflict management	**Definition:** the KSAOs needed to create and maintain a network of professional contacts within and outside of the organization, to build and maintain relationships, to work as an effective member of a team, and to manage conflict while supporting the organization.
Communication	
Sub-competencies: » Delivering messages » Exchanging organizational information » Listening	**Definition:** the KSAOs needed to effectively craft and deliver concise and informative communications, to listen to and address the concerns of others, and to transfer and translate information from one level or unit of the organization to another.
Global Mindset	
Sub-competencies: » Operating in a culturally diverse workplace » Operating in a global environment » Advocating for a culturally diverse and inclusive workplace	**Definition:** the KSAOs needed to value and consider the perspectives and backgrounds of all parties, to interact with others in a global context, and to promote a culturally diverse and inclusive workplace.

Business Cluster

Key components of Business behavioral competencies include the following:

» ensuring that HR contributes to the strategic direction of the organization

» understanding the business and the environment in which it operates

» designing and implementing business solutions to meet human capital needs

» contributing to and leading change management initiatives

» gathering and analyzing data to inform business decisions

Table 2.3. Business Cluster

Business Acumen	
Sub-competencies: » Business and competitive awareness » Business analysis » Strategic alignment	**Definition:** the KSAOs needed to understand the organization's operations, functions, and external environment, and to apply business tools and analyses that inform HR initiatives and operations consistent with the overall strategic direction of the organization.
Consultation	
Sub-competencies: » Evaluating business challenges » Designing HR solutions » Advising on HR solutions » Change management » Service excellence	**Definition:** the KSAOs needed to work with organizational stakeholders in evaluating business challenges and identifying opportunities for the design, implementation, and evaluation of change initiatives, and to build ongoing support for HR solutions that meet the changing needs of customers and the business.
Analytical Aptitude	
Sub-competencies: » Data advocate » Data gathering » Data analysis » Evidence-based decision-making	**Definition:** the KSAOs needed to collect and analyze qualitative and quantitative data and to interpret and promote findings that evaluate HR initiatives and inform business decisions and recommendations.

People Knowledge Domain

HR professionals need to know how to do the following:

» create and set the strategic direction of the HR function

» acquire and develop the talent necessary to pursue organizational goals

» maintain a satisfied and engaged workforce while minimizing unwanted employee turnover

» develop a total rewards program that maximizes the effectiveness of the organization's compensation and benefits

Table 2.4. Functional Areas in the People Knowledge Domain

HR Strategy
Definition: the activities necessary for developing, implementing, managing, and evaluating the strategic direction required to achieve organizational success and to create value for stakeholders.
Talent Acquisition
Definition: the activities involved in identifying, attracting, and building a workforce that meets the needs of the organization.
Employee Engagement & Retention
Definition: activities aimed at retaining talent, solidifying and improving the relationship between employees and the organization, creating a thriving and energized workforce, and developing effective strategies to address appropriate performance expectations from employees at all levels.
Learning & Development
Definition: activities that enhance the KSAOs and competencies of the workforce to meet the organization's current and future business needs.
Total Rewards
Definition: the design and implementation of compensation systems and benefits packages, which are used to attract and retain employees.

Organization Knowledge Domain

HR professionals need to know how to do the following:

» create an effective HR function that is fully aligned to organizational strategy

» enhance the effectiveness of the organization at large

» ensure that the organization's talent pool has the skills and capabilities to achieve organizational goals

» promote positive relationships with employees

» leverage technology to improve HR functioning

Table 2.5. Functional Areas in the Organization Knowledge Domain

Structure of the HR Function
Definition: the people, processes, and activities involved in the delivery of HR-related services that create and drive organizational effectiveness.
Organizational Effectiveness & Development
Definition: the overall structure and functionality of the organization, involving measurement of long- and short-term effectiveness and growth of people and processes and implementation of necessary organizational change initiatives.
Workforce Management
Definition: HR practices and initiatives that allow the organization to meet its talent needs and close critical gaps in competencies.
Employee & Labor Relations
Definition: any interactions between the organization and its employees regarding the terms and conditions of employment.
Technology Management
Definition: the use of existing, new, and emerging technologies to support the HR function and the development and implementation of policies and procedures governing the use of technologies in the workplace.

Workplace Knowledge Domain

HR professionals need to know how to do the following:

» manage a global workforce to achieve organizational objectives

» manage organizational risks and threats to the safety and security of employees

» contribute to the well-being and betterment of the community

» comply with applicable laws and regulations

Table 2.6. Functional Areas in the Workplace Knowledge Domain

Managing a Global Workforce
Definition: the role of the HR professional in managing global and mobile workforces to achieve organizational objectives.
Risk Management
Definition: the identification, assessment, and prioritization of risks, and the application of resources to minimize, monitor, and control the probability and impact of those risks accordingly.
Corporate Social Responsibility
Definition: the organization's commitment to operate ethically and contribute to economic development while improving the quality of life of the workforce and their families as well as of the local and global community.
U.S. Employment Law & Regulations
Definition: the knowledge and application of all relevant laws and regulations in the United States relating to employment—provisions that set the parameters and limitations for each HR functional area and for organizations overall. *Items from this functional area only appear on SHRM-CP exams delivered in the United States. These exam items are replaced by items from other Workplace knowledge functional areas for exams delivered outside of the United States.*

Organization of the SHRM BASK

Behavioral competencies facilitate the application of technical knowledge (i.e., HR Expertise). HR Expertise may be defined as the principles, practices, and functions of effective HR management.

Behavioral Competencies

Successful HR professionals must understand the behavioral components of HR practice in addition to being in command of technical HR knowledge. For each behavioral competency, the following information is provided:

» Definition of the competency.

» Key concepts describing the foundational knowledge for the competency.

» Sub-competencies applicable to the competency, with definitions.

» Proficiency indicators that apply to all HR professionals (i.e., early career through executive career levels) as well as those that apply primarily to advanced HR professionals (i.e., senior and executive career levels).

› Note that for the SHRM-CP, proficiency indicators for "all HR professionals" are the key ones to attend to.

Example Behavioral Competency: Diversity, Equity & Inclusion (DE&I)

To illustrate the structure of the behavioral competencies in the SHRM BASK, we are including the components of a single behavioral competency as an example.

Table 2.7. Diversity, Equity & Inclusion (DE&I)

Diversity, Equity & Inclusion (DE&I)	
Sub-competencies: » Creating a diverse and inclusive culture » Ensuring equity effectiveness » Connecting DE&I to organizational performance	**Definition:** the KSAOs needed to create a work environment in which all individuals are treated fairly and respectfully, have equal access to opportunities and resources, feel a sense of belonging, and use their unique backgrounds and characteristics to contribute fully to the organization's success.

Key Concepts from the DE&I Competency

» Characteristics of a dynamic workforce

> › Examples include multigenerational, multicultural, multilingual, multitalented, and multigendered

» Approaches to developing an inclusive workplace

> › Examples include executive sponsorship, leadership buy-in, allyship, unconscious-bias training, employee resource groups, mentorship, diversity metrics, psychological safety, and using preferred gender pronouns

» Workspace solutions

> › Examples include lactation room, prayer room, Braille and screen reader, closed captioning, wheelchair ramp, and gender-neutral restrooms

» Barriers to success involving conscious and unconscious bias

> › Examples include gender-based discrimination, racism (including systemic racism), stereotypes, ageism, ableism, ingroup/outgroup bias, affinity bias, gender identity bias, sexual orientation bias, social comparison bias, extroversion/introversion bias, neurodiversity bias, microaggressions, personal barriers such as imposter syndrome and identity covering, and cultural taxation

» Techniques to measure and increase equity

> › Examples include SHRM Empathy Index, diversity of employees at all organizational levels, pay audits, pay equity reports, pay transparency, and employee surveys

» Benefits and programs that support DE&I

> › Examples include caregiver options, workplace flexibility policies, paid leave options, tuition reimbursement programs, global festivities, and events calendar

» DE&I metrics

> › Examples include gender diversity, race diversity, retention rates for diverse employees, and diversity of external stakeholders

SHRM-CP Proficiency Indicators for All HR Professionals from the DE&I Competency

For sub-competency: Creating a Diverse and Inclusive Culture

» Recognizes, supports, and advocates on behalf of a diverse workforce with representation across race, gender, sexual orientation, ethnicity, religious beliefs, country of origin, education, abilities, and the intersectionality of the elements of diversity.

» Identifies and implements workspace solutions.

» Identifies, confronts, and addresses evidence of bias, stereotyping, microaggressions, and subtle acts of exclusion in the workplace.

» Provides professional development, mentoring, coaching, and guidance on cultural and diversity differences and practices to employees at all levels of the organization.

» Identifies and communicates the benefits of DE&I to employees and leaders.

» Develops and maintains knowledge of current trends and HR management best practices relating to DE&I.

» Implements HR programs, practices, and policies that encourage employees to embrace opportunities to work with those who possess diverse experiences and backgrounds.

» Supports a workplace culture and team that invite interpersonal risk taking, support mutual respect and trust, and do not embarrass or punish team members for speaking up.

For sub-competency: Ensuring Equity Effectiveness

» Contributes to the development and enhancement of an organizational culture that provides access, opportunity, and equity for all employees.

» Identifies opportunities to enhance the equity of organizational policies and procedures to all employees.

» Assesses equity using tools to determine the relationship among empathy, inclusion, and behavior.

» Implements and manages benefits and programs that support a diverse and equitable workforce.

» Consults with managers about behavioral distinctions between performance issues and DE&I differences.

» Partners with people managers to hire new employees from diverse groups across a variety of dimensions.

For sub-competency: Connecting DE&I to Organizational Performance

» Demonstrates support to internal and external stakeholders for the organization's DE&I efforts.

» Designs and executes effective DE&I initiatives to achieve business goals.

» Collects, reviews, analyzes, and effectively communicates DE&I metric results to show measurable effects on organizational objectives and productivity.

HR Expertise

In addition to the behavioral competencies, HR Expertise can be thought of as the single technical competency and is defined as the principles, practices, and functions of effective HR management.

Similar to the behavioral competencies, each functional knowledge area includes the following information:

» Definition of the functional area.

» Key concepts describing the knowledge specific to the functional area.

» Proficiency indicators that apply to all HR professionals (i.e., early career through executive career levels) as well as those that apply primarily to advanced HR professionals (i.e., senior and executive career levels).

> › Note that for the SHRM-CP, proficiency indicators for "all HR professionals" are the key ones to attend to.

Example Functional Area: Technology Management

To illustrate the structure of the functional areas in the SHRM BASK, we are including the components of a single functional area as an example.

The Technology Management functional area involves the use of existing, new, and emerging technologies to support the HR function and the development and implementation of policies and procedures governing the use of technologies in the workplace.

Key Concepts from the Technology Management Functional Area

» HR software and technology

> › Examples include applicant tracking system (ATS), human resource information system (HRIS), learning management system, performance management system, big data analytics software, collaboration software, blockchain, artificial intelligence, and machine learning

» Data and information management

> Examples include data integrity, confidentiality, security, disclosure, back-ups, cloud-based software, cybersecurity, and data retention

» Approaches to electronic self-service for HR and people management functions

> Examples include scheduling, time-keeping, contact information updates, and benefits enrollment

» Standards and policies for technology use

> Examples include bring-your-own-device policy, offsite network access policy, websites, computers for personal activity, internet messaging, and corporate and personal email

» Social media management

> Examples include internal social media platforms, social media policy, and branding

SHRM-CP Proficiency Indicators for All HR Professionals from the Technology Management Functional Area

» Implements and uses technology solutions that support or facilitate delivery of effective HR services and storage of critical candidate and employee data.

» Implements technology that integrates with and complements other enterprise information systems, software, and technology.

» Develops and implements organizational standards and policies for maintaining confidentiality of candidate and employee data, and limits access as appropriate.

» Uses technologies in a manner that protects workforce data.

» Provides guidance to stakeholders on effective standards and policies for use of technologies in the workplace.

» Coordinates and manages vendors implementing HR technology solutions.

» Uses technologies to collect, access, and analyze data and information to understand business challenges and recommend evidence-based solutions.

Section 3

The SHRM-CP Exam Blueprint

Not only does SHRM provide the potential content areas for the SHRM-CP exam in the SHRM BASK, SHRM also provides the actual breakdown of the numbers of exam items in the different content areas.

When measuring the three clusters of behavioral competencies, the exam includes close to equal representation from the different areas:

» **Leadership:** 17 percent of overall exam items

» **Business:** 16.5 percent of overall exam items

» **Interpersonal:** 16.5 percent of overall exam items

In addition, for the HR knowledge domains, People and Organization domains have more items than the Workplace domain. This difference is not surprising given the fact that Workplace only includes four functional areas, while People and Organization both include five functional areas.

» **People:** 18 percent of overall exam items

» **Organization:** 18 percent of overall exam items

» **Workplace:** 14 percent of overall exam items

Item Type

Situational Judgment (40%)
Foundational Knowledge (10%)

HR-Specific Knowledge (50%)

Behavioral Competency Clusters

Leadership (17%)
Business (16.5%)
Interpersonal (16.5%)

HR Knowledge Domains

People (18%)
Organization (18%)
Workplace (14%)

Figure 3.1. Distribution of Exam Items by Content and Exam Type

Self-Assessment for Your Exam Study Plan

Now that you have seen and started interacting with the SHRM BASK, you might feel a bit over-whelmed at the sheer volume of potential exam content. In fact, many SHRM-CP examinees are not sure what they should spend their time focused on and where they should start studying. To help diagnose your stronger and weaker areas and to direct your studying, we have put together this informal self-assessment for you.

Note that this is not a true assessment of your knowledge but an informal resource you can use to determine where you need the most help and could benefit most in studying.

As you go through this assessment, try to be honest with yourself about your level of expertise. In many cases, you might not have a good understanding of your own knowledge level. That is okay and completely expected. If you are unsure of the meaning of terms, that is probably an indicator that you are not very knowledgeable in the area.

As a reminder, you can find the complete version of the SHRM BASK at

> https://www.shrm.org/certification/about/BodyofAppliedSkillsandKnowledge/
> Pages/Download-SHRM-BASK.aspx

Instructions

Read the definition, the sub-competencies (for behavioral competencies), the key concepts, and the proficiency indicators for all HR professionals. This will involve obtaining the full SHRM BASK and using the definitions and various pieces of information in it.

Rate the competencies and knowledge areas based on your level of expertise by placing an **X** in the appropriate box.

Section 1: Rate Competencies in Leadership Cluster

	Rate Your Level of Expertise		
	Low	Moderate	High
Leadership & Navigation			
Sub-competencies: » Navigating the organization » Vision » Managing HR initiatives » Influence			
Ethical Practice			
Sub-competencies: » Personal integrity » Professional integrity » Ethical agent			
Diversity, Equity & Inclusion (DE&I)			
Sub-competencies: » Creating a diverse and inclusive culture » Ensuring equity effectiveness » Connecting DE&I to organizational performance			

Section 2: Rate Competencies in Interpersonal Cluster

	Rate Your Level of Expertise		
	Low	Moderate	High
Relationship Management			
Sub-competencies: » Networking » Relationship building » Teamwork » Negotiation » Conflict management			
Communication			
Sub-competencies: » Delivering messages » Exchanging organizational information » Listening			
Global Mindset			
Sub-competencies: » Operating in a culturally diverse workplace » Operating in a global environment » Advocating for a culturally diverse and inclusive workplace			

Section 3: Rate Competencies in Business Cluster

	Rate Your Level of Expertise		
	Low	Moderate	High
Business Acumen			
Sub-competencies: » Business and competitive awareness » Business analysis » Strategic alignment			
Consultation			
Sub-competencies: » Evaluating business challenges » Designing HR solutions » Advising on HR solutions » Change management » Service excellence			
Analytical Aptitude			
Sub-competencies: » Data advocate » Data gathering » Data analysis » Evidence-based decision-making			

Section 4: Rate Functional Areas in People Knowledge Domain

	Rate Your Level of Expertise		
	Low	Moderate	High
HR Strategy			
Talent Acquisition			
Employee Engagement & Retention			
Learning & Development			
Total Rewards			

Section 5: Rate Functional Areas in Organization Knowledge Domain

	Rate Your Level of Expertise		
	Low	Moderate	High
Structure of the HR Function			
Organizational Effectiveness & Development			
Workforce Management			
Employee & Labor Relations			
Technology Management			

Section 6: Rate Functional Areas in Workplace Knowledge Domain

	Rate Your Level of Expertise		
	Low	Moderate	High
Managing a Global Workforce			
Risk Management			
Corporate Social Responsibility			
U.S. Employment Law & Regulations			

Scoring the Assessment

Based on your self-ratings of expertise for each behavioral competency or functional area, you can interpret the results based on your ratings of expertise.

Low Expertise = Study Most: These are areas where you have little to no expertise/experience. If you primarily support employee relations and employee engagement, you may need to "study most" in areas such as talent acquisition or global mindset because you have little to no hands-on experience in this area.

Moderate Expertise = Study Some: These are areas where you have some expertise/experience, but you're not an expert. This could apply if you are a generalist with experience across many (or even most) competencies; you might have a surface-level knowledge of the competency, but you need to spend some time studying to better understand that competency outside of just your role or organization. If you used to work in a specific area but now perform a different set of job duties, this might apply too.

High Expertise = Review Only: These are the areas where you have the most expertise/experience. When you create your study plan, you don't want to spend too much time on these areas. Instead, you'll devote that time to studying the areas where you have more to learn. Note that these might be areas that you prefer to study or are most comfortable with. Because of this, you might have to fight the tendency to spend too much time in areas that you already know.

Interpreting the Assessment

You should now have twenty-three discrete ratings, one for each behavioral competency and functional area. Review your ratings and make notes about the terms, facts, and concepts that you need to learn or know more about so you can include them in your study plan.

It is important to review but not overstudy areas where your knowledge and familiarity with the content is already at a command-and-control level. Instead, focus your study efforts to improve your knowledge on the content with which you are least familiar. This means you should spend the majority of your study time on your "study most" areas, some time on your "study some" areas, and only a small amount of time on your "review" areas. Despite these recommendations, it is also important to note that the pass/fail decision for the exams are based on overall performance, rather than performance in each specific area. As a result, it is possible to pass the exam while performing rather poorly in a small number of subject areas.

Once you have your completed self-assessment, group together the items on your checklist that you can study together to identify study "blocks." As you sort items into groups, list the related terms and acronyms. Once you've identified your study blocks, you'll have the outline for your study plan.

Also, we should note that the reference list at the end of the BASK has many relevant books and other resources that are relevant for learning more about these competencies and functional areas. Remember that it is not a comprehensive list, but these are resources that have been approved by SHRM for item writers to use when creating exam items.

Create a SMART Study Plan

A *plan* is when a *want to* becomes a *how to*.

After going through the self-assessment and gaining some understanding of the areas of the SHRM-CP where you might need more studying, you should commit to making a plan for preparing for the exam. Although you might be able to follow a generic or informal plan, we know that the act of planning and committing is important for a lot of people to do things that are difficult.

One of the main reasons to focus on the study plan and schedule is the importance of writing things down. You are much more likely to take a goal/plan/commitment more seriously if you document it in a clear way. As such, we encourage you to take advantage of this workbook and use the templates provided in Appendix 2.

Here's how to create a study schedule that will fit into your life:[1]

1. Figure out how many hours you will need to cover everything on your study checklist. SHRM research shows that you should plan on spending at least eighty hours of preparation for the exam—although some people will need significantly more preparation time.

2. Start with the results of the self-assessment and plan your study time accordingly. You should also consider factors such as the extent of your HR experience and how quickly you tend to learn.

3. Determine how much of your time is already committed elsewhere. This will vary greatly between people. You should consider the time you need for family, work, exercise, personal care, and social activities, along with "downtime" and time for the unexpected, such as illness or a heavier-than-usual workload.

4. Decide how many hours of study time you will have available each week before the exam. If you plan to either form or join a study group or take an exam prep course, identify how many hours each week you will need for those activities. Then divide the remaining time into study sessions.

5. Determine a specific, achievable goal for each study session and identify the content you will study so you can achieve that goal. Keep in mind that you'll need more study time for some content than for others and build time into your schedule for practice exams so that you can assess what you are learning.

---

1. Alexander Alonso and Nancy Woolever, eds., *Ace Your SHRM Certification Exam: The Official SHRM Study Guide for the SHRM-CP® and SHRM-SCP® Exams*, 2nd ed. (Alexandria, VA: SHRM, 2022), 61–63.

6. Develop a realistic study schedule that shows your study sessions by date and time, the goal for each session, and the content you'll focus on during that session. Try to use this to make a realistic plan for an average of six to eight hours of study per week. Please note that there is no expectation of studying every day; however, it will be a good idea for you to plan on at least three days per week of some studying.

7. Create a week-by-week calendar that includes your scheduled activities for each day during your study period. Include time for family and friends, work (including your commute), scheduled appointments (doctors, dentists, etc.), exercise, and study sessions, study group meetings, and exam prep courses (if any).

Get Started on Your Study Schedule

Now step back and review your calendar:

How realistic is it?

Did you leave time for meals and personal care, as well as some "downtime" so you can rest and relax?

Did you leave buffer time in case of the unexpected?

If needed, go into your electronic calendar and set aside the time that you assigned to your studies.

Section 4

The SHRM-CP Practice Test

Introduction

This practice test includes forty items that were previously used on the SHRM-CP exam. These are different items than the ones that are used in the official SHRM study guide, *Ace Your SHRM Certification Exam*, and only include SHRM-CP items.

Similar to the real exam, this practice test is divided into separate sections that are composed of either knowledge items or situational judgment items. The first section contains a total of twelve knowledge and foundational knowledge items, the second section contains sixteen situational judgment items, and the third section contains another set of twelve knowledge and foundational knowledge items.

Because this practice test only contains forty items, it is not entirely representative of the entire blueprint that is used to build the SHRM-CP and SHRM-SCP exams. However, it is generally set up to cover all of the areas in the blueprint. This practice test will give you a taste of how the questions are structured on the exam and allow you to practice your test-taking strategies as you answer them.

To get a better sense of the real exams, SHRM recommends that you take the practice items during a timed period. We suggest you allot one and a half minutes per question (sixty minutes total) to gauge your ability to answer questions under the time constraints of the real exams.

One very important caution: do not assume that the ability to answer items on this forty-item practice test directly correlates to a passing score on the certification exam. This practice test is composed of less than one-third of the number of items on the SHRM-CP exams.

Additionally, the conditions in your at-home or in-office environment will not likely match the controlled environment in which a SHRM-CP exam is administered. For these reasons, the practice items are intended to give a preview of the structure and format of test questions. It is not appropriate to use these results to predict an outcome on your exam, and doing well on the practice test is not a guarantee of a passing result on your exam.

Additional information, including the answer key and rationales for the correct answers for knowledge and foundational knowledge items, appear at the end of the practice test. Answer keys are also provided for the situational judgment items (SJIs), but rationales are not provided due to the inherent nature of how these items are developed. Situational judgment items (SJIs) require judgment and decision-making to address workplace incidents, rather than relying on policy or law. All response options are actions that could be taken to respond to the situation, but there is only one "most effective" response. The most effective response is determined by diverse groups of experienced SHRM-certified HR professionals from around the globe who rate the effectiveness of each response. They also use the Proficiency Indicators outlined by the nine behavioral competencies in the SHRM BASK. Scoring of the most effective response is only done if the group of HR experts agree that this is the best response of all given alternatives.

When answering the SJI questions, do not base your response on an approach that is specific to your organization. Rather, use your understanding of HR best practice, which is documented in the SHRM BASK, to select your response.

To further challenge yourself in preparation for the exam, SHRM offers a comprehensive certification preparation resource, the SHRM Learning System®—which includes full-length SHRM-CP and SHRM-SCP exams full of previously used test items. In addition, the SHRM Learning System also includes an optional second exam at each certification level (for an additional fee). The SHRM Learning System is offered in a variety of formats—self-study and virtual or in-person seminars—and through partner universities that are authorized to teach the SHRM Learning System content.

Practice Test Questions

Section 1: This section has eight knowledge items (KIs).

1. The HR benefits specialist notices that employee benefits enrollment may not meet the minimum required for a positive return on investment. Which type of primary risk event would this most likely signify?

    A. Benefits strategy error

    B. Overpayment of premiums

    C. Plan design error

    D. Poor delivery of benefits information

2. A manufacturer revises its organizational structure to divide the work and employees by function. It also arranges employees such that they are accountable to a geographical manager. Which term best describes the organizational structure the manufacturer has adopted?

    A. Cross-functional

    B. Divisional

    C. Line

    D. Matrix

3. Which international governing body is responsible for promoting fair and equitable treatment of workers?

   A. World Trade Organization

   B. International Labor Organization

   C. Organization of Economic Cooperation and Development

   D. International Trade Union Confederation

4. Which HR function benefits most when an organization incorporates corporate social responsibility into its employee brand?

   A. Training and development

   B. Recruitment and retention

   C. Compensation and benefits

   D. Consulting and compliance

5. A company finishes conducting an engagement survey, and HR is tasked with next steps. How should HR handle the data in order to connect survey responses to the company's overall strategy and business goals?

   A. Review the data, benchmark against the external market, and provide findings to the CEO.

   B. Determine the organization's top desired outcomes, conduct an objective analysis of the data, and provide an action plan.

   C. Organize survey findings into low and high priority, communicate all data to staff, and align an action plan with employee needs.

   D. Provide top and bottom survey highlights to the CEO for review and input on results.

6. A company redesigns its comprehensive compliance program with the primary goal of encouraging employees to report ethical concerns. Which approach will best achieve the program's goal?

   A. Set up a confidential reporting system.

   B. Appoint a chief compliance officer.

   C. Create a detailed "common scenarios" guide.

   D. Launch a companywide compliance campaign.

7. An employee at a marketing firm files a harassment complaint and the HR manager must conduct an investigation. Which action should the HR manager take first?

    A. Develop a plan that identifies the purpose and scope of the investigation.

    B. Assure the accuser that confidentiality will be maintained.

    C. Interview the accuser, the accused, and potential witnesses.

    D. Ask the accuser for a written statement to document the complaint.

8. Which is an advantage of forced distribution ratings systems?

    A. Reduce contrast errors made by raters.

    B. Discourage leniency in performance ratings.

    C. Increase accuracy in performance reviews.

    D. Provide justification for placing employees in different rating groups.

Section 2: This section has eight situational judgment items (SJIs).

The following scenario goes with the next two items.

A distribution center has recently had a high level of turnover, including in the HR department. A new HR manager is hired. Within a few months on the job, the HR manager notices that the general manager at the location considers the HR manager's job to merely be one of managing paperwork with no strategic component. The general manager also takes HR issues straight to the HR director of the organization without talking to the HR manager first, despite the fact that the issues are all within the HR manager's job scope. The HR manager mentions these issues to a colleague in another distribution center and learns that other general managers in the organization treat their HR managers much better, but the colleague also mentions that this particular general manager has been known to behave like this. The HR manager also feels discouraged because the HR director is constantly criticizing the HR manager and never has anything positive to say about the HR manager's work.

9. The HR manager thinks the high turnover is due to the leadership practices of the general manager. The HR manager wants to implement an engagement survey to explore this and to help address other issues. The general manager is opposed to surveys. Which action should the HR manager take?

    A.   Provide data showing how many other companies use engagement surveys.

    B.   Share industry research on the value of an engagement strategy.

    C.   Present turnover trends to help the general manager understand the need for the engagement survey.

    D.   Ask for permission to conduct focus groups to understand engagement in the company.

The same scenario (repeated below) is also used for the next item.

A distribution center has recently had a high level of turnover, including in the HR department. A new HR manager is hired. Within a few months on the job, the HR manager notices that the general manager at the location considers the HR manager's job to merely be one of managing paperwork with no strategic component. The general manager also takes HR issues straight to the HR director of the organization without talking to the HR manager first, despite the fact that the issues are all within the HR manager's job scope. The HR manager mentions these issues to a colleague in another distribution center and learns that other general managers in the organization treat their HR managers much better, but the colleague also mentions that this particular general manager has been known to behave like this. The HR manager also feels discouraged because the HR director is constantly criticizing the HR manager and never has anything positive to say about the HR manager's work.

10. The HR manager would like to be seen as a strategic partner, rather than just someone who handles HR-related paperwork. Which action should the HR manager take to help the general manager see the HR manager as a strategic partner?

    A. Ask the HR director to talk to the general manager about the value of the HR manager as a strategic partner.

    B. Demonstrate knowledge of business functions through comments in meetings.

    C. Ask the general manager what the HR manager can do to be seen as a strategic partner.

    D. Ask the general manager what the HR manager can do to assist in meeting the organizational goals for the fiscal year.

The following scenario goes with the next three items.

A large organization is comprised of several divisions with similar organizational structures that include support staff, specialists, and supervisors. Many of the organization's employees, especially new hires, are 20 to 30 years old. The HR manager who supports one of the divisions notices several growing trends. Requests from managers for position reclassifications are rising. Support staff are increasingly requesting to become specialists, and specialists are asking to become supervisors. Furthermore, turnover is increasing. The organization gives annual merit raises and has a policy granting midyear raises only if an employee's job responsibilities change significantly. Divisions are unable to modify the salary ranges or the salary raise policy, although they can create new jobs and titles within the existing structure. However, salary increases do not seem to satisfy employees who are seeking not only salary growth but increased authority and recognition. To retain staff, managers are adding responsibilities to employees' jobs in an attempt to promote movement to a higher level. Similarly, managers have given some specialists supervisory authority over several positions as a way to move them into the supervisory classification. As a consequence, some divisions are now comprised of more hierarchical levels. After considering the issue, the HR manager suggests that the best solution is to create a career ladder with a senior-level position for each job classification. This strategy would allow for career growth within a role without requiring a move to a higher-level job.

11. Which factor is most critical for the HR manager to consider in developing the proposed career ladder solution?

    A. Entry-level compensation requirements for the new positions

    B. Use of career ladders in competing organizations

    C. Division-specific needs for higher-level positions

    D. Selection processes for new positions

The same scenario (repeated below) is also used for the next item.

A large organization is comprised of several divisions with similar organizational structures that include support staff, specialists, and supervisors. Many of the organization's employees, especially new hires, are 20 to 30 years old. The HR manager who supports one of the divisions notices several growing trends. Requests from managers for position reclassifications are rising. Support staff are increasingly requesting to become specialists, and specialists are asking to become supervisors. Furthermore, turnover is increasing. The organization gives annual merit raises and has a policy granting midyear raises only if an employee's job responsibilities change significantly. Divisions are unable to modify the salary ranges or the salary raise policy, although they can create new jobs and titles within the existing structure. However, salary increases do not seem to satisfy employees who are seeking not only salary growth but increased authority and recognition. To retain staff, managers are adding responsibilities to employees' jobs in an attempt to promote movement to a higher level. Similarly, managers have given some specialists supervisory authority over several positions as a way to move them into the supervisory classification. As a consequence, some divisions are now comprised of more hierarchical levels. After considering the issue, the HR manager suggests that the best solution is to create a career ladder with a senior-level position for each job classification. This strategy would allow for career growth within a role without requiring a move to a higher-level job.

12. Which action best describes what the HR manager should do to engage employees and division managers during the development of a proposed solution?

    A. Determine the satisfaction levels of promoted employees.

    B. Gather employee input on salary increases and compensation programs.

    C. Have division managers meet with employees to explain the proposed strategy.

    D. Clarify long-term career development expectations of employees and managers.

The same scenario (repeated below) is also used for the next item.

A large organization is comprised of several divisions with similar organizational structures that include support staff, specialists, and supervisors. Many of the organization's employees, especially new hires, are 20 to 30 years old. The HR manager who supports one of the divisions notices several growing trends. Requests from managers for position reclassifications are rising. Support staff are increasingly requesting to become specialists, and specialists are asking to become supervisors. Furthermore, turnover is increasing. The organization gives annual merit raises and has a policy granting midyear raises only if an employee's job responsibilities change significantly. Divisions are unable to modify the salary ranges or the salary raise policy, although they can create new jobs and titles within the existing structure. However, salary increases do not seem to satisfy employees who are seeking not only salary growth but increased authority and recognition. To retain staff, managers are adding responsibilities to employees' jobs in an attempt to promote movement to a higher level. Similarly, managers have given some specialists supervisory authority over several positions as a way to move them into the supervisory classification. As a consequence, some divisions are now comprised of more hierarchical levels. After considering the issue, the HR manager suggests that the best solution is to create a career ladder with a senior-level position for each job classification. This strategy would allow for career growth within a role without requiring a move to a higher-level job.

13. What information should the HR manager convey to senior leadership to advance the proposed career ladder solution?

　　A. Testimonials from individual employees supporting the proposal

　　B. Results of recent employee satisfaction surveys

　　C. Estimates of return on investment associated with the proposal

　　D. Number of employees promoted within the past three years

The following scenario goes with the next three items.

An international manufacturing company creates a joint venture with sixteen manufacturing facilities that are geographically dispersed across four countries. The joint venture is currently managed under a single executive team that demands reliable and ethical business practices. The HR director for the international manufacturing company is partnering with the finance and business unit leaders for the joint venture to implement an internal audit function that reports directly to the executive team. Because of the obstacles associated with hiring in multiple international locations as well as time and budget limitations, the HR director and executive team agree to hire a qualified internal audit director to lead auditor recruiting. One joint venture partner refers a candidate with multinational accounting and management experience. The HR director hires the referred candidate for the internal audit director position. The new internal audit director starts immediately and begins traveling to the manufacturing facilities to review safety and business practices. Although auditor recruiting is within the director's role, no additional auditors are hired. After several months, the VP of accounting informs the HR director of continuous travel expenses incurred by the internal audit director with no return home between audit assignments. Submitted expenses include living expenses, as well as leisure activities, weekend meals, entertainment, and dry cleaning. The VP of accounting reveals that the internal audit director's expenses also include travel costs incurred for the internal audit director's spouse. The company decides to launch an investigation into excessive charges on the internal audit director's expense reports.

14. What is the first step the HR director should take to understand what the organization requires from the internal audit director in the expense reporting process?

    A.   Interview the internal audit director about the expense reporting process.

    B.   Audit the expense reports acquired by the VP of accounting.

    C.   Review the job description and recruiting materials shared with the internal audit director.

    D.   Review the expense report policies in the employee handbook.

The same scenario (repeated below) is also used for the next item.

An international manufacturing company creates a joint venture with sixteen manufacturing facilities that are geographically dispersed across four countries. The joint venture is currently managed under a single executive team that demands reliable and ethical business practices. The HR director for the international manufacturing company is partnering with the finance and business unit leaders for the joint venture to implement an internal audit function that reports directly to the executive team. Because of the obstacles associated with hiring in multiple international locations as well as time and budget limitations, the HR director and executive team agree to hire a qualified internal audit director to lead auditor recruiting. One joint venture partner refers a candidate with multinational accounting and management experience. The HR director hires the referred candidate for the internal audit director position. The new internal audit director starts immediately and begins traveling to the manufacturing facilities to review safety and business practices. Although auditor recruiting is within the director's role, no additional auditors are hired. After several months, the VP of accounting informs the HR director of continuous travel expenses incurred by the internal audit director with no return home between audit assignments. Submitted expenses include living expenses, as well as leisure activities, weekend meals, entertainment, and dry cleaning. The VP of accounting reveals that the internal audit director's expenses also include travel costs incurred for the internal audit director's spouse. The company decides to launch an investigation into excessive charges on the internal audit director's expense reports.

15. During the investigation, the internal audit director becomes frustrated and challenges the findings, stating that they were never told that travel with a spouse and the associated expenses that incurred as a result were not allowed. What is the next step for the HR director to take in resolving this issue?

    A. Suggest placing the internal audit director on a performance improvement plan.

    B. Present the key findings from the investigation to the company's employment attorney and ask for counsel.

    C. Consult with the CFO and VP of accounting about the expense report details and performance expectations.

    D. Mediate a conflict resolution discussion between the internal audit director and the executive team.

The same scenario (repeated below) is also used for the next item.

An international manufacturing company creates a joint venture with sixteen manufacturing facilities that are geographically dispersed across four countries. The joint venture is currently managed under a single executive team that demands reliable and ethical business practices. The HR director for the international manufacturing company is partnering with the finance and business unit leaders for the joint venture to implement an internal audit function that reports directly to the executive team. Because of the obstacles associated with hiring in multiple international locations as well as time and budget limitations, the HR director and executive team agree to hire a qualified internal audit director to lead auditor recruiting. One joint venture partner refers a candidate with multinational accounting and management experience. The HR director hires the referred candidate for the internal audit director position. The new internal audit director starts immediately and begins traveling to the manufacturing facilities to review safety and business practices. Although auditor recruiting is within the director's role, no additional auditors are hired. After several months, the VP of accounting informs the HR director of continuous travel expenses incurred by the internal audit director with no return home between audit assignments. Submitted expenses include living expenses, as well as leisure activities, weekend meals, entertainment, and dry cleaning. The VP of accounting reveals that the internal audit director's expenses also include travel costs incurred for the internal audit director's spouse. The company decides to launch an investigation into excessive charges on the internal audit director's expense reports.

16. The HR director recommends that the company develop a code of conduct to ensure that all employees know the company's business ethics guidelines. What should the HR director do to reinforce its message about business ethics and conduct in order to encourage upward communication without fear of retaliation?

    A. Implement an anonymous ethics hotline to take employee calls and complaints.

    B. Disseminate the code to all employees and require all employees to sign and acknowledge it.

    C. Hold an all-employees meeting at each location to explain the policy to employees.

    D. Prepare posters, messages, and collateral materials reinforcing the ethics guidelines.

Section 3: This section has eight knowledge items (KIs).

17. In e-recruiting, which individual is considered an applicant?

    A.   An individual who has completed an onboarding process

    B.   An individual who is researching the organization

    C.   An individual who was recently terminated

    D.   An individual who expresses interest in an advertised position

18. Which statement best describes the primary purpose of a balanced scorecard strategy?

    A.   Score the performance of HR within an organization.

    B.   Enable the measurement of employee performance.

    C.   Provide a historical overview of physical and tangible assets.

    D.   Measure customer and employee satisfaction and loyalty.

19. Which is the most cost-effective HR strategy to reduce unconscious bias in hiring?

    A.   Have HR staff remove identifying information from resumes before passing them on to the hiring managers.

    B.   Hire a consultant to remove identifying information from resumes before passing them on to the hiring managers.

    C.   Eliminate identifying information from resumes by requesting that candidates not include it when applying.

    D.   Buy a recruiting platform that removes identifying information.

20. Which component of a succession plan provides information on individuals who have promotion potential?

    A.   Transition procedure

    B.   Talent pool

    C.   Training program

    D.   Workforce proposal

21. Which learning approach would be most effective in an organization comprised of employees with diverse skills and experiences?

    A. Cooperative

    B. Distance

    C. Hands-on

    D. Blended

22. Which is a major disadvantage of implementing a fully integrated HRIS?

    A. Creating silos of information within the organization

    B. Customizing to meet the needs of each function

    C. Ensuring the integrity of the data

    D. Restricting user access to irrelevant HR data

23. Which action should an HR manager take to best facilitate the repatriation process?

    A. Set up clear policies and procedures to assist repatriates with re-entry and utilize the international skills and knowledge of expatriates upon return.

    B. Acknowledge the amount of confusion faced during the repatriation process and provide career guidance to repatriates to help put their expertise to work.

    C. Communicate with expatriates before their assignments end and present accurate information to minimize disappointments.

    D. Ensure that expatriates are well-compensated during assignments and that have minimal financial concerns upon re-entry.

24. Which learning and development technique uses practice and feedback to help learners build their self-efficacy prior to using a newly acquired skill to perform daily tasks?

    A. Experiential program

    B. Role-play

    C. Group discussion

    D. Lecture

Section 4: This section has eight situational judgment items (SJIs).

The following scenario goes with the next two items.

An employee receives positive performance reviews for three consecutive years but anticipates a negative performance review for the current year due to challenges with performing job duties. The employee is aware that company policy prohibits the delivery of performance reviews to employees while absent for an extended period of time and, therefore, intentionally enters an office, locks the door, refuses to exit, and reports feeling sad and worthless to anyone who expresses their concern. The HR manager convinces the employee to exit and, as expected, grants a sabbatical, which gives the employee time off for rest and relaxation. While the employee is away from work, the employee's co-workers express to the HR manager their concerns about the employee's emotional well-being and their worries about their safety upon the employee's return. The HR manager promises to handle the issue in a professional manner. The company has another policy granting employees full decision-making authority regarding when it is appropriate to return to work following time off for rest and relaxation for emotional stress. The HR manager communicates this policy to the employee. Soon thereafter, the employee sets a date to return to work and requests a flexible work arrangement until completion of a program for employees with stress-related medical conditions.

25. Which action is best for the HR manager to take to reduce the concern among co-workers regarding the employee's return to work?

    A. Meet with the employee's co-workers to reassure them that the employee will not return to work until the employee's emotional stability returns to normal.

    B. Discuss with the employee the possible challenges associated with re-establishing relationships with co-workers given their awareness of the employee's circumstances.

    C. Conduct a general information session for concerned co-workers on coping with work-related stress, maintaining work–family balance, and interacting with emotionally unstable co-workers.

    D. Explain the policy stating how decisions are made regarding an employee's return to work following time off for issues related to stress and emotional instability.

The same scenario (repeated below) is also used for the next item.

An employee receives positive performance reviews for three consecutive years but anticipates a negative performance review for the current year due to challenges with performing job duties. The employee is aware that company policy prohibits the delivery of performance reviews to employees while absent for an extended period of time and, therefore, intentionally enters an office, locks the door, refuses to exit, and reports feeling sad and worthless to anyone who expresses their concern. The HR manager convinces the employee to exit and, as expected, grants a sabbatical, which gives the employee time off for rest and relaxation. While the employee is away from work, the employee's co-workers express to the HR manager their concerns about the employee's emotional well-being and their worries about their safety upon the employee's return. The HR manager promises to handle the issue in a professional manner. The company has another policy granting employees full decision-making authority regarding when it is appropriate to return to work following time off for rest and relaxation for emotional stress. The HR manager communicates this policy to the employee. Soon thereafter, the employee sets a date to return to work and requests a flexible work arrangement until completion of a program for employees with stress-related medical conditions.

26. Which argument is best for the HR manager to make to ensure that the employee's co-workers understand why the company supports the employee's return to work?

    A. The employee has agreed to a flexible work schedule until the employee is ready to return to work.

    B. The rest and relaxation program helps employees to recover from stress and emotional instability.

    C. Company policy states that employees are able to independently decide when to return to work.

    D. The employee's actions are due to concerns about a personal matter and will not occur in the future.

The following scenario goes with the next two items.

A security contractor provides services to a large manufacturing plant that include security patrol staff, vehicles, and cameras. Security staff are considered temporary employees and the terms of their employment are managed by the plant's HR office, which is located in a different part of the country. Daily plant operations are loud and dangerous, involving the use of heavy industrial equipment and a constant stream of large trucks delivering raw materials. Security staff patrol the plant facility at all times and are required to wear protective gear over their eyes, ears, and heads. The HR director, who has never visited the plant, receives an email from a plant manager reporting several incidents of the same patrol officer nearly being injured by moving equipment. The plant manager believes the patrol officer's hearing is impaired and requests termination paperwork for the patrol officer.

27. The HR director reviews the patrol officer's job description and discovers that it does not align with the actual job environment and does not list any physical requirements. What should the HR director do to address the misalignment?

    A. Advise the plant manager to conduct focus groups with employees to assess current physical requirements.

    B. Advise the plant manager to schedule all patrol officers for an exam to measure their hearing abilities.

    C. Notify the contractor that security staff may need to undergo physical fitness testing in the future.

    D. Ask legal to determine if the patrol officer has a viable litigation case against the company.

The same scenario (repeated below) is also used for the next item.

A security contractor provides services to a large manufacturing plant that include security patrol staff, vehicles, and cameras. Security staff are considered temporary employees and the terms of their employment are managed by the plant's HR office, which is located in a different part of the country. Daily plant operations are loud and dangerous, involving the use of heavy industrial equipment and a constant stream of large trucks delivering raw materials. Security staff patrol the plant facility at all times and are required to wear protective gear over their eyes, ears, and heads. The HR director, who has never visited the plant, receives an email from a plant manager reporting several incidents of the same patrol officer nearly being injured by moving equipment. The plant manager believes the patrol officer's hearing is impaired and requests termination paperwork for the patrol officer.

28. What should the HR director do to demonstrate support for the patrol officer's well-being while maintaining the plant's operational efficiency?

    A.   Request authorization from senior leadership to conduct an on-site visit of the plant.

    B.   Conduct teleconferences with all plant managers to discuss their concerns about employee safety.

    C.   Submit a request to senior leadership to allocate funding for an all-hands training on plant safety.

    D.   Conduct one-on-one meetings with a sample of employees to discuss critical safety risks.

The following scenario goes with the next two items.

Favorable market conditions exist for the statistical software division of a software company. However, the company at large experiences an overall decline in sales and revenue. In response, the company hires a general manager to lead the statistical software division with an expectation that the statistical software division's positive performance will improve the overall company sales and revenue. For two years, attrition levels increase, and, as a result, the company awards no base salary increases and annual bonuses during that period. Currently, some of the company's key technical positions remain unfilled, and the recruiting team reports that this is attributable to base salary levels that are below market rates. To achieve the statistical software division's financial targets for the year, the general manager must hire additional sales and technical personnel. The CEO requests a monthly meeting with the general manager and HR director to review the statistical software division's business and hiring results. The HR director assigns a high-performing recruiter to work with the general manager and business team to support the hiring requirements. The HR director recommends that the recruiter hold periodic meetings with the hiring managers to review progress against hiring goals. The day before the monthly meeting with the CEO, the general manager, obviously frustrated with the HR director over the lack of hiring results, demands that an external recruiting firm replace the recruiter. On the morning of the meeting with the CEO, the CFO issues a companywide email announcing the suspension of onboarding for new hires.

29. Which action taken by the HR director to address the general manager's concerns about lack of hiring results is most likely to yield the most effective outcome?

    A. Attend the periodic recruiting status meetings with the general manager and team to resolve prospective issues.

    B. Develop a recruiting remediation plan to apologize to the general manager for the lack of recruiting results.

    C. Hire additional external recruiting resources to target the specialized technical talent needed by the division.

    D. Replace the assigned recruiter immediately to demonstrate rapid resolution of the general manager's concerns.

The same scenario (repeated below) is also used for the next item.

Favorable market conditions exist for the statistical software division of a software company. However, the company at large experiences an overall decline in sales and revenue. In response, the company hires a general manager to lead the statistical software division with an expectation that the statistical software division's positive performance will improve the overall company sales and revenue. For two years, attrition levels increase, and, as a result, the company awards no base salary increases and annual bonuses during that period. Currently, some of the company's key technical positions remain unfilled, and the recruiting team reports that this is attributable to base salary levels that are below market rates. To achieve the statistical software division's financial targets for the year, the general manager must hire additional sales and technical personnel. The CEO requests a monthly meeting with the general manager and HR director to review the statistical software division's business and hiring results. The HR director assigns a high-performing recruiter to work with the general manager and business team to support the hiring requirements. The HR director recommends that the recruiter hold periodic meetings with the hiring managers to review progress against hiring goals. The day before the monthly meeting with the CEO, the general manager, obviously frustrated with the HR director over the lack of hiring results, demands that an external recruiting firm replace the recruiter. On the morning of the meeting with the CEO, the CFO issues a companywide email announcing the suspension of onboarding for new hires.

30. Which action is key for the HR director to incorporate into a strategic talent management plan to close unfilled key positions?

    A. Hire an external consultant to recruit candidates with highly specialized technical talent and intrinsic motivation.

    B. Require the statistical software management team to dedicate adequate time for interviewing and hiring.

    C. Develop a social media strategy for the statistical software division to promote the company and open positions.

    D. Evaluate where needed skills may reside across the company to offer internal transfer and training opportunities.

The following scenario goes with the next two items.

The HR manager of a large appliance company receives a complaint from an employee in the sales department. The complaint reports that the sales manager, who the employee reports to, does not complete work properly or on time. The sales manager blames others for the manager's own mistakes and takes credit for the successes of others on the team without recognizing their work. The HR manager reviews the sales manager's performance files and is surprised because all reviews are entirely positive. The HR manager does, however, notice that turnover has increased on the team.

31. When the HR manager shares the complaint with the sales manager's department director, the director wants to dismiss the complaint since the sales manager's reviews from peers and supervisors have always been high. What approach should the HR manager take to convince the director that performance reviews may be inaccurate?

    A. Explain the various types of rater biases and how they can be reflected in performance reviews.

    B. Remind the director that the direct report perspective is not captured in the performance reviews.

    C. Say that peers may be providing favorable ratings in exchange for high ratings for themselves.

    D. Provide research on the various problems facing performance reviews.

The same scenario (repeated below) is also used for the next item.

The HR manager of a large appliance company receives a complaint from an employee in the sales department. The complaint reports that the sales manager, who the employee reports to, does not complete work properly or on time. The sales manager blames others for the manager's own mistakes and takes credit for the successes of others on the team without recognizing their work. The HR manager reviews the sales manager's performance files and is surprised because all reviews are entirely positive. The HR manager does, however, notice that turnover has increased on the team.

32. The HR manager determines the complaints were valid, and the employee subsequently complains that, due to an inaccurate performance review, the employee did not receive a salary bonus this year. What should the HR manager do in response?

    A. Obtain a salary bonus for the employee who complained.

    B. Ask the employee why the lack of salary bonus was not mentioned previously.

    C. Ask the sales manager to re-assess all bonus decisions from the previous year.

    D. Conduct an audit of all the sales manager's compensation decisions for the previous year.

Section 5: This section has eight knowledge items (KIs).

33. Which practice is best to follow when implementing lean thinking?

    A.   Ensuring senior managers champion and lead the initiative.

    B.   Developing lean thinking systems and processes specific to each business unit.

    C.   Focusing primarily on sales staff with significant levels of customer interaction.

    D.   Benchmarking progress against productivity metrics for previous years.

34. A company facing financial difficulties needs all frontline employees to stay home from work temporarily and not be paid, in a final effort to avoid layoffs. Which action is most effective in communicating this workforce change?

    A.   Deliver individual memos to all impacted employees, followed by phone calls to the impacted employees and their supervisors.

    B.   Facilitate multiple in-person sessions with company leadership to explain the decision, followed by individual meetings with all impacted employees and their supervisors.

    C.   Post a notification and explanation on the company's intranet, followed by individual letters emailed to all impacted employees.

    D.   Send a companywide email announcement from the CEO, followed by a meeting with all employees and the company leadership.

35. Which is a benefit of an ethical working self-concept in shaping the culture of the workplace?

    A.   Simplifies the communication of expectations for employees to act in a manner that is consistent with organizational values.

    B.   Impacts employees' supervisors' willingness to take responsibility for ethical mistakes that impact performance of daily work tasks.

    C.   Establishes a precedent for justice in the policies and practices that affect employees and their work.

    D.   Makes it easier to administer tools for assessing the ethical character of those with whom employees work.

36. A company has a highly specialized project that requires an individual with specific skills in an area of IT software coding who will need to be retained for approximately six months. In which employment category does this individual belong?

    A. Independent contractor

    B. Full-time regular employee

    C. Part-time regular employee

    D. Seasonal employee

37. Which task should be accomplished in the onboarding process during an employee's first week on the job?

    A. Provide the employee with training on skills necessary to do the job.

    B. Complete post-offer activities and paperwork such as reference checks and criminal background documents.

    C. Familiarize the employee with the job and the company's work policies and benefits.

    D. Conduct assessments to determine if the employee has attributes needed to be successful.

38. Of what type of organizational statement is "Supportable growth; enabled people; commitment and conviction" an example?

    A. Vision

    B. Mission

    C. Value

    D. Goal

39. Which best explains how designing jobs with high levels of job autonomy ultimately results in high levels of job satisfaction among employees?

    A. Stimulation of job responsibility

    B. Motivation of meaningful work

    C. Information and knowledge of results

    D. Clarification of working conditions

40. Which program is most effective for helping full-time employees manage commuting patterns and educational, volunteer, and wellness activities?

   A.   Telework

   B.   Compressed workweek

   C.   Flextime

   D.   Job sharing

Appendix 1

The SHRM-CP Practice Test Answers

Section 1: This section has eight knowledge items (KIs).

1. The HR benefits specialist notices that employee benefits enrollment may not meet the minimum required for a positive return on investment. Which type of primary risk event would this most likely signify?

    A. Benefits strategy error

    B. Overpayment of premiums

    C. Plan design error

    D. Poor delivery of benefits information

Domain	Difficulty	Key
Workplace	Hard	A

Rationale	
A.	Benefits strategy error is correct because it is a primary risk event and a good strategy which meant to achieve an overall aim which did not happen in this case.
B.	Overpayment of premiums is incorrect because this is a secondary event risk of a benefit strategy error.
C.	Plan design error is incorrect because this is a secondary event risk and is the failure to consider potential errors.
D.	Poor delivery of benefits information is incorrect because it is an example of risk that should be considered in the strategy plan.

S/IS = X

2. A manufacturer revises its organizational structure to divide the work and employees by function. It also arranges employees such that they are accountable to a geographical manager. Which term best describes the organizational structure the manufacturer has adopted?

   A. Cross-functional

   B. Divisional

   C. Line

   D. Matrix

Domain	Difficulty	Key
Organization	Hard	D

Rationale

A. Cross-functional is incorrect because it consists of groups or teams made up of different disciplines across the organization.

B. Divisional is incorrect because it most often divides work and employees by output. It can also divide by market or region.

C. Line is incorrect because in this case, direct lines of authority extend from the top manager to the lowest level of the organization.

D. Matrix is correct because a matrix structure combines the functional and divisional organizational structures and typically has an employee reporting to two managers who are jointly responsible for the employee's performance. Typically, one manager works in an administrative function, such as finance, HR, information technology, sales, or marketing, and the other works in a business unit related to a product, service, customer, or geography.

S/IS = X

3. Which international governing body is responsible for promoting fair and equitable treatment of workers?

    A. World Trade Organization

    B. International Labor Organization

    C. Organization of Economic Cooperation and Development

    D. International Trade Union Confederation

Domain	Difficulty	Key
Organization	Easy	B

Rationale

A. World Trade Organization (WTO) is incorrect. The WTO has begun to address the issue of labor standards and the basic rights of labor organizations, but is mainly focused on the economic and developmental aspects of their affiliate nations. The WTO defers to the ILO for core labor standards.

B. International Labor Organization (ILO) is the correct answer. The ILO's primary focus it to improve labor codes and rights by outlining standards and good practices regarding employment practices. The ILO provides the benchmark in which firms and governments are measured by. This includes political sensitivities and lesser publicized labor practices that are now informed by ILO standards.

C. Organization of Economic Cooperation and Development (OECD) is incorrect The OECD addresses globalization issues through economic, environmental and social policy. While the OECD is mainly focused on the economic and developmental aspects of their affiliate nations, they do increasingly address employment issues.

D. International Trade Union Confederation is incorrect. Even though the organization does advocate for workers rights, it is done indirectly through international cooperation between trade unions. Its main areas of activity include the following: trade union and human rights; economy, society and the workplace; equality and nondiscrimination; and international solidarity.

S/15 = ✓

4. Which HR function benefits most when an organization incorporates corporate social responsibility into its employee brand?

   A. Training and development

   B. Recruitment and retention

   C. Compensation and benefits

   D. Consulting and compliance

Domain	Difficulty	Key
Workplace	Easy	B

Rationale

A. Training and development is incorrect because it can be an internal CSR activity for employees. However, it is not impacted to the same extent as recruitment and retention because training activities are not seen as CSR initiatives by employees, nor communicated by the company in that way.

B. Recruitment and retention is the correct answer because corporate social responsibility (CSR) contributes to building a company's brand and this helps in attracting and retaining talent. Employees tend to see a company as more favorable if it works on CSR initiatives.

C. Compensation and benefits is incorrect because CSR doesn't refer to monetary and non-monetary benefits passed on by a firm to its employees based on their performance.

D. Consulting and compliance is incorrect because CSR may be done as a result of this function in order to comply with regulations or law in a country but would not impact their overall work.

S/IS = ✓

5. A company finishes conducting an engagement survey, and HR is tasked with next steps. How should HR handle the data in order to connect survey responses to the company's overall strategy and business goals?

    A. Review the data, benchmark against the external market, and provide findings to the CEO.

    B. Determine the organization's top desired outcomes, conduct an objective analysis of the data, and provide an action plan.

    C. Organize survey findings into low and high priority, communicate all data to staff, and align an action plan with employee needs.

    D. Provide top and bottom survey highlights to the CEO for review and input on results.

Domain	Difficulty	Key
Business	Somewhat Easy	B

Rationale

A. Review the data, benchmark . . . is incorrect because although benchmarking is a valuable metric and can help executives examine engagement surveys, it is only collected data and does not provide a way to connect the data to the company's business outcomes or overall strategy. The data must also be compared objectively to find the cause-and-effect of the relationship within the company, not externally.

B. Determine the organization's top desired outcomes . . . is correct because HR should first determine the organization's top desired outcomes, then conduct an objective analysis of the data and provide an action plan. This option includes three of the six steps in processing data and driving HR strategy by connecting HR directly to business outcomes.

C. Organize the survey findings . . . is incorrect because in order for HR to connect the data to how it impacts business, it must align to the organization's needs and not individual employees.

D. Provide top and bottom . . . is incorrect because reviewing data without action is only collecting information and not analyzing it to meet the organization's objectives. Sending the data to the CEO is incorrect, as there is no action plan by HR and it is not connected to the company's strategy.

5/15 = ✓

6. A company redesigns its comprehensive compliance program with the primary goal of encouraging employees to report ethical concerns. Which approach will best achieve the program's goal?

   A. Set up a confidential reporting system.

   B. Appoint a chief compliance officer.

   C. Create a detailed "common scenarios" guide.

   D. Launch a companywide compliance campaign.

Domain	Difficulty	Key
Organization	Somewhat Easy	A

Rationale

A. Set up a confidential reporting system is the correct answer. Employees are generally more comfortable using reporting systems administered by external third parties because of confidentiality issues. When employees believe the reporting system is truly anonymous, they are more likely to report and findings because the fear of a negative impact on their performance evaluations or employment is severely diminished

B. Appoint a chief compliance officer is incorrect. While appointing a chief compliance officer would increase awareness of the company's commitment of ethics & compliance, it would not guarantee encouragement for employees to report. Some employees may not be comfortable speaking to the chief compliance officer because many fear what could happen to their future careers or employment.

C. Create a detailed "common scenarios" guide is incorrect. The common scenarios guide cannot detail a blueprint for defining the many nuances of situations. Providing common scenarios could encourage employees to only apply those types of situations to their ethical thinking and would not necessarily encourage all types of ethical reports.

D. Launch a companywide compliance campaign is incorrect. The communication of the campaign may increase the awareness of ethics & compliance, but it won't guarantee increasing the comfort for employees to report. This is part of launching a successful internal ethical reporting system, but does not best achieve the goal for encouraging reporting.

S/15 = ✓

7. An employee at a marketing firm files a harassment complaint and the HR manager must conduct an investigation. Which action should the HR manager take first?

    A. Develop a plan that identifies the purpose and scope of the investigation.

    B. Assure the accuser that confidentiality will be maintained.

    C. Interview the accuser, the accused, and potential witnesses.

    D. Ask the accuser for a written statement to document the complaint.

Domain	Difficulty	Key
Workplace	Hard	A

Rationale

A. Develop a plan that identifies the . . . is correct because the plan will map out the process, including who will need to be interviewed and what documentation will be necessary.

B. Assure the accuser that confidentiality . . . is incorrect because it cannot be guaranteed as information gathered may be necessary to share at some point in time with appropriate parties.

C. Interview the accuser . . . is incorrect because although the accuser will be part of the interview process, the HR manager will want to develop a plan first and ensure all necessary information is gathered during the interview.

D. Ask the accuser for a written . . . is incorrect because the complaint has already been filed and will provide sufficient information to help develop a plan that identifies the purpose and scope of the investigation; however, a full written statement may be part of that plan.

 S|IS = ✓

8. Which is an advantage of forced distribution ratings systems?

   A.   Reduce contrast errors made by raters.

   B.   Discourage leniency in performance ratings.

   C.   Increase accuracy in performance reviews.

   D.   Provide justification for placing employees in different rating groups.

Domain	Difficulty	Key
People	Hard	B

Rationale

A.   Reduce contrast errors made by raters is incorrect because contrast errors are a type of rating error in which the evaluation of a target person in a group is affected by the level of performance of others in the group. When the others are high in performance, there may be a tendency to rate the target lower than is accurate for their performance due to comparisons to their peers. When the others are low in performance, there may be a tendency to rate the target higher than is accurate.

B.   Discourage leniency in performance ratings is correct because forced distribution rating systems force you to produce a bell curve with roughly 10 percent high performers, 10 percent poor performers, and everyone else falling in the middle, preventing managers from rating everyone highly or in a lenient way.

C.   Increase accuracy in performance reviews is incorrect because force rankings make the entire employee population follow a set distribution which may not be a correct representation of the true distribution of how employees perform.

D.   Provide justification for placing employees in different rating groups is incorrect because a forced distribution places employees in different performance buckets based on comparisons to each other. There does not have to be a cited reason for the placement or evaluation against any performance standards for making the decisions.

S/IS = X

Section 2: This section has eight situational judgment items (SJIs).

Situational judgment items (SJIs) require judgment and decision-making to address workplace incidents, rather than relying on policy or law. All response options are actions that could be taken to respond to the situation, but there is only one "most effective" response. The most effective response is determined by diverse groups of experienced SHRM-certified HR professionals from around the globe who rate the effectiveness of each response. They also use the Proficiency Indicators outlined by the nine behavioral competencies in the SHRM BASK. Scoring of the most effective response is only done if the group of HR experts agree that this is the best response of all given alternatives.

When answering the SJI questions, do not base your response on an approach that is specific to your organization. Rather, use your understanding of HR best practice, which is documented in the SHRM BASK, to select your response.

The following scenario goes with the next two items.

A distribution center has recently had a high level of turnover, including in the HR department. A new HR manager is hired. Within a few months on the job, the HR manager notices that the general manager at the location considers the HR manager's job to merely be one of managing paperwork with no strategic component. The general manager also takes HR issues straight to the HR director of the organization without talking to the HR manager first, despite the fact that the issues are all within the HR manager's job scope. The HR manager mentions these issues to a colleague in another distribution center and learns that other general managers in the organization treat their HR managers much better, but the colleague also mentions that this particular general manager has been known to behave like this. The HR manager also feels discouraged because the HR director is constantly criticizing the HR manager and never has anything positive to say about the HR manager's work.

9. The HR manager thinks the high turnover is due to the leadership practices of the general manager. The HR manager wants to implement an engagement survey to explore this and to help address other issues. The general manager is opposed to surveys. Which action should the HR manager take?

   A. Provide data showing how many other companies use engagement surveys.

   B. Share industry research on the value of an engagement strategy.

   C. Present turnover trends to help the general manager understand the need for the engagement survey.

   D. Ask for permission to conduct focus groups to understand engagement in the company.

Domain	Difficulty	Key
Leadership	Somewhat Easy	C

5/15 = ✓

10. The HR manager would like to be seen as a strategic partner, rather than just someone who handles HR-related paperwork. Which action should the HR manager take to help the general manager see the HR manager as a strategic partner?

   A. Ask the HR director to talk to the general manager about the value of the HR manager as a strategic partner.

   B. Demonstrate knowledge of business functions through comments in meetings.

   C. Ask the general manager what the HR manager can do to be seen as a strategic partner.

   D. Ask the general manager what the HR manager can do to assist in meeting the organizational goals for the fiscal year.

Domain	Difficulty	Key
Business	Somewhat Easy	D

5/15 = X

The following scenario goes with the next three items.

A large organization is comprised of several divisions with similar organizational structures that include support staff, specialists, and supervisors. Many of the organization's employees, especially new hires, are 20 to 30 years old. The HR manager who supports one of the divisions notices several growing trends. Requests from managers for position reclassifications are rising. Support staff are increasingly requesting to become specialists, and specialists are asking to become supervisors. Furthermore, turnover is increasing. The organization gives annual merit raises and has a policy granting midyear raises only if an employee's job responsibilities change significantly. Divisions are unable to modify the salary ranges or the salary raise policy, although they can create new jobs and titles within the existing structure. However, salary increases do not seem to satisfy employees who are seeking not only salary growth but increased authority and recognition. To retain staff, managers are adding responsibilities to employees' jobs in an attempt to promote movement to a higher level. Similarly, managers have given some specialists supervisory authority over several positions as a way to move them into the supervisory classification. As a consequence, some divisions are now comprised of more hierarchical levels. After considering the issue, the HR manager suggests that the best solution is to create a career ladder with a senior-level position for each job classification. This strategy would allow for career growth within a role without requiring a move to a higher-level job.

11. Which factor is most critical for the HR manager to consider in developing the proposed career ladder solution?

A.   Entry-level compensation requirements for the new positions

B.   Use of career ladders in competing organizations

C.   Division-specific needs for higher-level positions

D.   Selection processes for new positions

Domain	Difficulty	Key
Business	Somewhat Easy	C

5/15 = X

12. Which action best describes what the HR manager should do to engage employees and division managers during the development of a proposed solution?

    A.   Determine the satisfaction levels of promoted employees.

    B.   Gather employee input on salary increases and compensation programs.

    C.   Have division managers meet with employees to explain the proposed strategy.

    D.   Clarify long-term career development expectations of employees and managers.

Domain	Difficulty	Key
Interpersonal	Somewhat Hard	D

S|IS = X

13. What information should the HR manager convey to senior leadership to advance the proposed career ladder solution?

    A.   Testimonials from individual employees supporting the proposal

    B.   Results of recent employee satisfaction surveys

    C.   Estimates of return on investment associated with the proposal

    D.   Number of employees promoted within the past three years

Domain	Difficulty	Key
Business	Somewhat Easy	C

S|IS = ✓

The following scenario goes with the next three items.

An international manufacturing company creates a joint venture with sixteen manufacturing facilities that are geographically dispersed across four countries. The joint venture is currently managed under a single executive team that demands reliable and ethical business practices. The HR director for the international manufacturing company is partnering with the finance and business unit leaders for the joint venture to implement an internal audit function that reports directly to the executive team. Because of the obstacles associated with hiring in multiple international locations as well as time and budget limitations, the HR director and executive team agree to hire a qualified internal audit director to lead auditor recruiting. One joint venture partner refers a candidate with multinational accounting and management experience. The HR director hires the referred candidate for the internal audit director position. The new internal audit director starts immediately and begins traveling to the manufacturing facilities to review safety and business practices. Although auditor recruiting is within the director's role, no additional auditors are hired. After several months, the VP of accounting informs the HR director of continuous travel expenses incurred by the internal audit director with no return home between audit assignments. Submitted expenses include living expenses, as well as leisure activities, weekend meals, entertainment, and dry cleaning. The VP of accounting reveals that the internal audit director's expenses also include travel costs incurred for the internal audit director's spouse. The company decides to launch an investigation into excessive charges on the internal audit director's expense reports.

14. What is the first step the HR director should take to understand what the organization requires from the internal audit director in the expense reporting process?

   A.   Interview the internal audit director about the expense reporting process.

   B.   Audit the expense reports acquired by the VP of accounting.

   C.   Review the job description and recruiting materials shared with the internal audit director.

   D.   Review the expense report policies in the employee handbook.

Domain	Difficulty	Key
Business	Somewhat Easy	D

S/15 = ✓

15. During the investigation, the internal audit director becomes frustrated and challenges the findings, stating that they were never told that travel with a spouse and the associated expenses that incurred as a result were not allowed. What is the next step for the HR director to take in resolving this issue?

    A. Suggest placing the internal audit director on a performance improvement plan.

    B. Present the key findings from the investigation to the company's employment attorney and ask for counsel.

    C. Consult with the CFO and VP of accounting about the expense report details and performance expectations.

    D. Mediate a conflict resolution discussion between the internal audit director and the executive team.

Domain	Difficulty	Key
Leadership	Somewhat Hard	C

S|IS = ✓

16. The HR director recommends that the company develop a code of conduct to ensure that all employees know the company's business ethics guidelines. What should the HR director do to reinforce its message about business ethics and conduct in order to encourage upward communication without fear of retaliation?

    A. Implement an anonymous ethics hotline to take employee calls and complaints.

    B. Disseminate the code to all employees and require all employees to sign and acknowledge it.

    C. Hold an all-employee meeting at each location to explain the policy to employees.

    D. Prepare posters, messages, and collateral materials reinforcing the ethics guidelines.

Domain	Difficulty	Key
Leadership	Hard	A

S|IS = X

Section 3: This section has eight knowledge items (KIs).

17. In e-recruiting, which individual is considered an applicant?

A.   An individual who has completed an onboarding process

B.   An individual who is researching the organization

C.   An individual who was recently terminated

D.   An individual who expresses interest in an advertised position

Domain	Difficulty	Key
Organization	Easy	D

Rationale

A.   An individual who has completed an onboarding process is incorrect. If an individual has completed an onboarding process, they have passed the application portion of the employment process therefore is no longer considered an applicant. The four stages of the employment process are recruiting, interviewing, selection, and orientation.

B.   An individual who is researching the organization is incorrect. This individual may have interest in the organization, but has not expressed interest in any particular role the organization has. This would not qualify them as an internet applicant, as none of the elements of an internet application are met. The four elements are as follows: expressing interest in employment through the internet or electronic means, considered for employment in a particular role, expression of interest indicates basic qualifications are met for the position, individual at no point expresses lack of desire in the position prior to receiving an offer.

C.   An individual who was recently terminated is incorrect. While this individual may begin searching for new employment, their lack of expression of interest in any roles does not qualify them as an applicant. This individual could still be sourced and contacted by a recruiter, but does not meet the four elements of an internet applicant. The four elements are as follows: expressing interest in employment through the internet or electronic means, considered for employment in a particular role, expression of interest indicates basic qualifications are met for the position, individual at no point expresses lack of desire in the position prior to receiving an offer.

D.   An individual who expresses interest in an advertised position is correct. There are four elements that determine if an individual is an internet applicant. The four elements are as follows: expressing interest in employment through the internet or electronic means, considered for employment in a particular role, expression of interest indicates basic qualifications are met for the position, individual at no point expresses lack of desire in the position prior to receiving an offer.

5/15 = ✓

18. Which statement best describes the primary purpose of a balanced scorecard strategy?

    A. Score the performance of HR within an organization.

    B. Enable the measurement of employee performance.

    C. Provide a historical overview of physical and tangible assets.

    D. Measure customer and employee satisfaction and loyalty.

Domain	Difficulty	Key
Organization	Hard	D

Rationale

A. Score the performance of HR within an organization is incorrect as the balanced score-card is not a tool to measure HR effectiveness, but instead presents possible solutions to improve financial, innovative, customer-wise, and internal operating procedures.

B. Enable the measurement of employee performance is incorrect as a balanced scorecard is not a performance management tool and does not measure employee performance.

C. Provide a historical overview of physical and tangible assets is incorrect because balanced scorecards measure financial but not the physical assets.

D. Measure customer and employee satisfaction and loyalty is correct as the balanced scorecard identifies internal operations to help external outcomes and customer satisfaction.

$S/IS = X$

19. Which is the most cost-effective HR strategy to reduce unconscious bias in hiring?

    A.   Have HR staff remove identifying information from resumes before passing them on to the hiring managers.

    B.   Hire a consultant to remove identifying information from resumes before passing them on to the hiring managers.

    C.   Eliminate identifying information from resumes by requesting that candidates not include it when applying.

    D.   Buy a recruiting platform that removes identifying information.

Domain	Difficulty	Key
Workplace	Hard	C

Rationale

A.   Have HR staff remove . . . is incorrect because it will increase the team's workload, which is likely to incur overtime costs.

B.   Hire a consultant to remove . . . is incorrect because this is an additional expense and consultancy fees are typically high.

C.   Eliminate identifying information from resumes by requesting . . . is correct because it does not cost the company anything to ask candidates to remove their own identifying information.

D.   Buy a recruiting platform . . . is incorrect because it an additional cost and typically has high initial set up costs.

$5/15 = X$

20. Which component of a succession plan provides information on individuals who have promotion potential?

    A.   Transition procedure

    B.   Talent pool

    C.   Training program

    D.   Workforce proposal

Domain	Difficulty	Key
Organization	Easy	B

Rationale

A.   Transition procedure is incorrect because it is a process of replacing a leader with someone decided upon.

B.   Talent pool is correct because it represents a database of suitable candidates who can replace leaders when they leave or retire.

C.   Training program is incorrect because the scope is to close a skills gap.

D.   Workforce proposal is incorrect because a workforce proposal is not a component of succession planning.

S/15 = ✓

21. Which learning approach would be most effective in an organization comprised of employees with diverse skills and experiences?

    A.   Cooperative

    B.   Distance

    C.   Hands-on

    D.   Blended

Domain	Difficulty	Key
Business	Somewhat Easy	D

Rationale

A.   Cooperative is incorrect because it is not a method of learning.

B.   Distance is incorrect because it focuses on availability of expert trainers and cost-effectiveness to reach geographically dispersed participants and focuses mainly on virtual classroom courses.

C.   Hands-on is incorrect because it is face-to-face and is only one method.

D.   Blended is correct because it is a combination of different methods of learning. It is effective in an organization with employees with diverse skills and experiences.

S/IS = X

22. Which is a major disadvantage of implementing a fully integrated HRIS?

   A. Creating silos of information within the organization

   B. Customizing to meet the needs of each function

   C. Ensuring the integrity of the data

   D. Restricting user access to irrelevant HR data

Domain	Difficulty	Key
Organization	Hard	B

Rationale

A. Creating silos of information within the organization is incorrect because it is an advantage as a fully integrated HRIS will coordinate all function to operate as one.

B. Customizing to meet the needs of each function is correct because it creates a major disadvantage in the implementation process as it is difficult to get all functions aligned and customizing needs for each function.

C. Ensuring the integrity of the data is incorrect because this selects the appropriate system and service providers after performing a risk-based validation.

D. Restricting user access to irrelevant HR data is incorrect because it is an implicit action especially when working with sensitive data.

S/15 = ✓

23. Which action should an HR manager take to best facilitate the repatriation process?

  A. Set up clear policies and procedures to assist repatriates with re-entry and utilize the international skills and knowledge of expatriates upon return.

  B. Acknowledge the amount of confusion faced during the repatriation process and provide career guidance to repatriates to help put their expertise to work.

  C. Communicate with expatriates before their assignments end and present accurate information to minimize disappointments.

  D. Ensure that expatriates are well-compensated during assignments and that have minimal financial concerns upon re-entry.

Domain	Difficulty	Key
Workplace	Somewhat Easy	A

Rationale

  A. Set up clear policies and procedures . . . is correct as it's essential to have a set roadmap and procedure to follow when helping expatriates repatriate back home, mainly to utilize their international skills and knowledge.

  B. Acknowledge the amount . . . is incorrect as it doesn't help facilitate the repatriation process; instead, it just helps career guidance to come back to work.

  C. Communicate with expatriates . . . is incorrect as communication alone won't set a roadmap and detailed process of repatriation and maintaining international skills.

  D. Ensure that expatriates are . . . is incorrect because financial support will not facilitate the repatriation process; it will only cover financial concerns upon re-entry.

S/15 = ✓

24. Which learning and development technique uses practice and feedback to help learners build their self-efficacy prior to using a newly acquired skill to perform daily tasks?

    A.   Experiential program

    B.   Role-play

    C.   Group discussion

    D.   Lecture

Domain	Difficulty	Key
People	Easy	B

Rationale

A.   Experiential program is incorrect because it is a learning process through experiences and reflection.

B.   Role-play is correct because it is a learning technique that requires active participation from learners who play different roles and collaborate with each other to solve a problem and emphasizes understanding of different perspectives in real-world situations.

C.   Group discussion is incorrect because it is set of individuals who exchange information or ideas.

D.   Lecture is incorrect because it does not allow for much discussion or involvement from learners.

S|IS = ✓

Section 4: This section has eight situational judgment items (SJIs).

Situational judgment items (SJIs) require judgment and decision-making to address workplace incidents, rather than relying on policy or law. All response options are actions that could be taken to respond to the situation, but there is only one "most effective" response. The most effective response is determined by diverse groups of experienced SHRM-certified HR professionals from around the globe who rate the effectiveness of each response. They also use the Proficiency Indicators outlined by the nine behavioral competencies in the SHRM BASK. Scoring of the most effective response is only done if the group of HR experts agree that this is the best response of all given alternatives.

When answering the SJI questions, do not base your response on an approach that is specific to your organization. Rather, use your understanding of HR best practice, which is documented in the SHRM BASK, to select your response.

The following scenario goes with the next two items.

An employee receives positive performance reviews for three consecutive years but anticipates a negative performance review for the current year due to challenges with performing job duties. The employee is aware that company policy prohibits the delivery of performance reviews to employees while absent for an extended period of time and, therefore, intentionally enters an office, locks the door, refuses to exit, and reports feeling sad and worthless to anyone who expresses their concern. The HR manager convinces the employee to exit and, as expected, grants a sabbatical, which gives the employee time off for rest and relaxation. While the employee is away from work, the employee's co-workers express to the HR manager their concerns about the employee's emotional well-being and their worries about their safety upon the employee's return. The HR manager promises to handle the issue in a professional manner. The company has another policy granting employees full decision-making authority regarding when it is appropriate to return to work following time off for rest and relaxation for emotional stress. The HR manager communicates this policy to the employee. Soon thereafter, the employee sets a date to return to work and requests a flexible work arrangement until completion of a program for employees with stress-related medical conditions.

25. Which action is best for the HR manager to take to reduce the concern among co-workers regarding the employee's return to work?

    A. Meet with the employee's co-workers to reassure them that the employee will not return to work until the employee's emotional stability returns to normal.

    B. Discuss with the employee the possible challenges associated with reestablishing relationships with co-workers given their awareness of the employee's circumstances.

    C. Conduct a general information session for concerned co-workers on coping with work-related stress, maintaining work-family balance, and interacting with emotionally unstable co-workers.

    D. Explain the policy stating how decisions are made regarding an employee's return to work following time off for issues related to stress and emotional instability.

Domain	Difficulty	Key
Interpersonal	Somewhat Hard	C

S/IS = ✓

26. Which argument is best for the HR manager to make to ensure that the employee's co-workers understand why the company supports the employee's return to work?

    A. The employee has agreed to a flexible work schedule until the employee is ready to return to work.

    B. The rest and relaxation program helps employees to recover from stress and emotional instability.

    C. Company policy states that employees are able to independently decide when to return to work.

    D. The employee's actions are due to concerns about a personal matter and will not occur in the future.

Domain	Difficulty	Key
Interpersonal	Hard	B

S/IS = X

The following scenario goes with the next two items.

A security contractor provides services to a large manufacturing plant that include security patrol staff, vehicles, and cameras. Security staff are considered temporary employees and the terms of their employment are managed by the plant's HR office, which is located in a different part of the country. Daily plant operations are loud and dangerous, involving the use of heavy industrial equipment and a constant stream of large trucks delivering raw materials. Security staff patrol the plant facility at all times and are required to wear protective gear over their eyes, ears, and heads. The HR director, who has never visited the plant, receives an email from a plant manager reporting several incidents of the same patrol officer nearly being injured by moving equipment. The plant manager believes the patrol officer's hearing is impaired and requests termination paperwork for the patrol officer.

27. The HR director reviews the patrol officer's job description and discovers that it does not align with the actual job environment and does not list any physical requirements. What should the HR director do to address the misalignment?

    A.   Advise the plant manager to conduct focus groups with employees to assess current physical requirements.

    B.   Advise the plant manager to schedule all patrol officers for an exam to measure their hearing abilities.

    C.   Notify the contractor that security staff may need to undergo physical fitness testing in the future.

    D.   Ask legal to determine if the patrol officer has a viable litigation case against the company.

Domain	Difficulty	Key
Business	Somewhat Hard	A

S/15 = X

28. What should the HR director do to demonstrate support for the patrol officer's well-being while maintaining the plant's operational efficiency?

    A.   Request authorization from senior leadership to conduct an on-site visit of the plant.

    B.   Conduct teleconferences with all plant managers to discuss their concerns about employee safety.

    C.   Submit a request to senior leadership to allocate funding for an all-hands training on plant safety.

    D.   Conduct one-on-one meetings with a sample of employees to discuss critical safety risks.

Domain	Difficulty	Key
Leadership	Somewhat Hard	A

S/15 = X

The following scenario goes with the next two items.

Favorable market conditions exist for the statistical software division of a software company. However, the company at large experiences an overall decline in sales and revenue. In response, the company hires a general manager to lead the statistical software division with an expectation that the statistical software division's positive performance will improve the overall company sales and revenue. For two years, attrition levels increase and, as a result, the company awards no base salary increases and annual bonuses during that period. Currently, some of the company's key technical positions remain unfilled, and the recruiting team reports that this is attributable to base salary levels that are below market rates. To achieve the statistical software division's financial targets for the year, the general manager must hire additional sales and technical personnel. The CEO requests a monthly meeting with the general manager and HR director to review the statistical software division's business and hiring results. The HR director assigns a high-performing recruiter to work with the general manager and business team to support the hiring requirements. The HR director recommends that the recruiter hold periodic meetings with the hiring managers to review progress against hiring goals. The day before the monthly meeting with the CEO, the general manager, obviously frustrated with the HR director over the lack of hiring results, demands that an external recruiting firm replace the recruiter. On the morning of the meeting with the CEO, the CFO issues a companywide email announcing the suspension of onboarding for new hires.

29. Which action taken by the HR director to address the general manager's concerns about lack of hiring results is most likely to yield the most effective outcome?

    A. Attend the periodic recruiting status meetings with the general manager and team to resolve prospective issues.

    B. Develop a recruiting remediation plan to apologize to the general manager for the lack of recruiting results.

    C. Hire additional external recruiting resources to target the specialized technical talent needed by the division.

    D. Replace the assigned recruiter immediately to demonstrate rapid resolution of the general manager's concerns.

Domain	Difficulty	Key
Interpersonal	Somewhat Easy	A

S/IS = ✓

30. Which action is key for the HR director to incorporate into a strategic talent management plan to close unfilled key positions?

    A.   Hire an external consultant to recruit candidates with highly specialized technical talent and intrinsic motivation.

    B.   Require the statistical software management team to dedicate adequate time for interviewing and hiring.

    C.   Develop a social media strategy for the statistical software division to promote the company and open positions.

    D.   Evaluate where needed skills may reside across the company to offer internal transfer and training opportunities.

Domain	Difficulty	Key
Business	Somewhat Easy	D

S/15 = ✓

The following scenario goes with the next two items.

The HR manager of a large appliance company receives a complaint from an employee in the sales department. The complaint reports that the sales manager, who the employee reports to, does not complete work properly or on time. The sales manager blames others for the manager's own mistakes and takes credit for the successes of others on the team without recognizing their work. The HR manager reviews the sales manager's performance files and is surprised because all reviews are entirely positive. The HR manager does, however, notice that turnover has increased on the team.

31. When the HR manager shares the complaint with the sales manager's department director, the director wants to dismiss the complaint since the sales manager's reviews from peers and supervisors have always been high. What approach should the HR manager take to convince the director that performance reviews maybe inaccurate?

    A. Explain the various types of rater biases and how they can be reflected in performance reviews.

    B. Remind the director that the direct report perspective is not captured in the performance reviews.

    C. Say that peers may be providing favorable ratings in exchange for high ratings for themselves.

    D. Provide research on the various problems facing performance reviews.

Domain	Difficulty	Key
Leadership	Somewhat Hard	B

S/IS = X

32. The HR manager determines the complaints were valid, and the employee subsequently complains that, due to an inaccurate performance review, the employee did not receive a salary bonus this year. What should the HR manager do in response?

    A. Obtain a salary bonus for the employee who complained.

    B. Ask the employee why the lack of salary bonus was not mentioned previously.

    C. Ask the sales manager to re-assess all bonus decisions from the previous year.

    D. Conduct an audit of all the sales manager's compensation decisions for the previous year.

Domain	Difficulty	Key
Leadership	Easy	D

S/IS = ✓

Section 5: This section has eight knowledge items (KIs).

33. Which practice is best to follow when implementing lean thinking?

    A.   Ensuring senior managers champion and lead the initiative.

    B.   Developing lean thinking systems and processes specific to each business unit.

    C.   Focusing primarily on sales staff with significant levels of customer interaction.

    D.   Benchmarking progress against productivity metrics for previous years.

Domain	Difficulty	Key
People	Hard	A

Rationale

A.   Ensuring senior managers champion and lead the initiative is correct because senior managers set the tone and ensure that each person understands the work, is actively engaged, challenged to improve processes to deliver value, eliminate waste, and increase profitability.

B.   Developing lean thinking systems and processes specific to each business unit is incorrect because systems and processes may overlap, and this will be one of the steps in the lean thinking process.

C.   Focusing primarily on sales staff with significant levels of customer interaction is incorrect because lean thinking is about continuous learning and improvement capabilities across the organization not just the sales staff.

D.   Benchmarking progress against productivity metrics for previous years is incorrect because company objectives and projects may change year over year.

S/15 = X

34. A company facing financial difficulties needs all frontline employees to stay home from work temporarily and not be paid, in a final effort to avoid layoffs. Which action is most effective in communicating this workforce change?

   A. Deliver individual memos to all impacted employees, followed by phone calls to the impacted employees and their supervisors.

   B. Facilitate multiple in-person sessions with company leadership to explain the decision, followed by individual meetings with all impacted employees and their supervisors.

   C. Post a notification and explanation on the company's intranet, followed by individual letters emailed to all impacted employees.

   D. Send a companywide email announcement from the CEO, followed by a meeting with all employees and the company leadership.

Domain	Difficulty	Key
Interpersonal	Easy	B

Rationale

A. Deliver individual memos . . . is incorrect because it lacks the personal touch needed in a time of crisis. Although the action may be efficient it is not effective.

B. Facilitate multiple in-person . . . is the correct answer because the decision impacts all frontline employees, and a consistent message cascades through leadership and individual meetings to clear any additional worries and to secure the current employees.

C. Post a notification and explanation . . . is incorrect because not all company's employees are impacted, and this type of communication is not targeting those affected and it may create confusion.

D. Send a companywide email . . . is incorrect as this decision is only for frontline employees and this action of companywide announcement should be taken after all impacted employees are informed in individual meetings with their supervisors.

S|IS = ✓

35. Which is a benefit of an ethical working self-concept in shaping the culture of the workplace?

    A.   Simplifies the communication of expectations for employees to act in a manner that is consistent with organizational values.

    B.   Impacts employees' supervisors' willingness to take responsibility for ethical mistakes that impact performance of daily work tasks.

    C.   Establishes a precedent for justice in the policies and practices that affect employees and their work.

    D.   Makes it easier to administer tools for assessing the ethical character of those with whom employees work.

Domain	Difficulty	Key
Workplace	Easy	A

Rationale

A. Simplifies the communication of . . . is correct because when a lack of strategy is prevalent in an organization, self-concept can aid in creating common strategy and purpose and therefore simplify communication.

B. Impacts employees' supervisors' willingness . . . is incorrect because in ethical communication, communication about ethical and unethical behavior and its consequences must be made available to managers and employees so they can both act responsibly, not just supervisors.

C. Establishes a precedent for . . . is incorrect because if employees perceive the organization's policies and practices or those of its leaders as unfair or unjust, distrust will cripple performance. There is no precedent for fairness, only that it is expected.

D. Makes it easier to administer . . . is incorrect because the tool can only be as effective as how it is disseminated and used. Ethical self-concept cannot guarantee that tools are used effectively.

S/15 = X

36. A company has a highly specialized project that requires an individual with specific skills in an area of IT software coding who will need to be retained for approximately six months. In which employment category does this individual belong?

    A. Independent contractor

    B. Full-time regular employee

    C. Part-time regular employee

    D. Seasonal employee

Domain	Difficulty	Key
People	Easy	A

Rationale

A. Independent contractor is correct because they are highly skilled workers contracted by organizations to work on specific projects for defined periods of time, typically less than one year, and are not a permanent part of the company's staff.

B. Full-time regular employee is incorrect because they are a full-time, permanent member of the company's staff and are not typically assigned to one specific project or a defined or limited period of time with the company.

C. Part-time regular employee is incorrect because they are a part-time, but permanent member of the company's staff and are not typically assigned to one specific project or a defined or limited period of time with the company.

D. Seasonal employee is incorrect because they are hired for a particular period of time during busy or "peak" seasons in the business, but they are not required to have a highly specialized set of skills in a specific area.

S/15 = ✓

37. Which task should be accomplished in the onboarding process during an employee's first week on the job?

   A.   Provide the employee with training on skills necessary to do the job.

   B.   Complete post-offer activities and paperwork such as reference checks and criminal background documents.

   C.   Familiarize the employee with the job and the company's work policies and benefits.

   D.   Conduct assessments to determine if the employee has attributes needed to be successful.

Domain	Difficulty	Key
People	Easy	C

Rationale

A.   Provide the employee with . . . is incorrect because employees should have most, if not all, of the skills necessary to complete their job prior to accepting the job. Specific skills and training needed for the role can be learned on the job.

B.   Complete post-offer activities . . . is incorrect because this should be completed prior to employee onboarding.

C.   Familiarize the employee with . . . is correct because familiarizing employees with the company's culture can take weeks or months depending on the organization, but it is the right first step during employee orientation and onboarding. This helps them get acquainted with the organization's polices and culture, it helps them know and understand the growth pattern of the organization especially as it concerns them. It could also serve as a motivation for employees to give their best to the organization.

D.   Conduct assessments to determine . . . is incorrect because this should be conducted prior to employee onboarding.

S/15 = ✓

38. Of what type of organizational statement is "Supportable growth; enabled people; commitment and conviction" an example?

    A. Vision

    B. Mission

    C. Value

    D. Goal

Domain	Difficulty	Key
People	Hard	C

Rationale

A. Vision is incorrect because a vision is a forward-looking statement that creates a mental picture of the ideal state an organization wishes to achieve.

B. Mission is incorrect because a mission is a brief explanation of the organization's reason for existing.

C. Value is correct because it is a list of core principles that guide and direct the organization and its culture.

D. Goal is incorrect because a goal is a statement of achievement with a defined end time.

S/IS = X

39. Which best explains how designing jobs with high levels of job autonomy ultimately results in high levels of job satisfaction among employees?

    A.   Stimulation of job responsibility

    B.   Motivation of meaningful work

    C.   Information and knowledge of results

    D.   Clarification of working conditions

Domain	Difficulty	Key
People	Hard	A

Rationale

A. Stimulation of job responsibility is correct because autonomy requires an employee to take on a greater degree of ownership in, and responsibility for, doing a job. This results in high intrinsic motivation.

B. Motivation of meaningful work is incorrect because autonomy does not dictate the degree of meaning that is associated with a particular job.

C. Information and knowledge of results is incorrect because autonomy does not provide any information or knowledge about results for the job.

D. Clarification of working conditions is incorrect because autonomy does not provide any information about the working conditions of a job.

S//S = X

40. Which program is most effective for helping full-time employees manage commuting patterns and educational, volunteer, and wellness activities?

    A. Telework

    B. Compressed workweek

    C. Flextime

    D. Job sharing

Domain	Difficulty	Key
People	Easy	C

Rationale

A. Telework is incorrect because it is a work arrangement where an employee works from home or away from the usual workplace through telecommunications technology.

B. Compressed workweek is incorrect because, in a compressed workweek, an employee works fewer days but longer work hours each day. The advantage of a compressed work schedule is that the employee gets time off during the week or fortnight and still gets paid a full salary. The disadvantage is that it can be stressful working a very long day and might affect the general well-being of the employee which is why the flextime option is the most effective in managing commuting time and wellness activities.

C. Flextime is the correct because this work arrangement offers employees the flexibility to alter either the start or end time of the workday or alter both. Though employees are still required to work the same number of scheduled hours as they would under a traditional schedule, flextime offers employees the opportunity to manage commuting time better and also help with work-life balance.

D. Job sharing is incorrect because it is a work arrangement where two or more employees share the responsibilities of one full-time position typically with prorated salary or paid time off.

S/IS = ✓

Appendix 2

Twelve-Week Study Schedule Template

We have provided a set of study schedule templates to guide your SHRM-CP exam preparation. Please use these spaces to create your plan and write it down.

Planned Test Date with Prometric: _____

Study Week 1: _____

Weekly Goal: This week, I will...

_____

_____

_____

_____

	Planned Time	Study Focus
Sunday		
Monday		
Tuesday		
Wednesday		
Thursday		
Friday		
Saturday		

Study Week 2: _____

Weekly Goal: This week, I will...

_____

_____

_____

_____

	Planned Time	Study Focus
Sunday		
Monday		
Tuesday		
Wednesday		
Thursday		
Friday		
Saturday		

Study Week 3: _____

Weekly Goal: This week, I will...

_____

_____

_____

_____

	Planned Time	Study Focus
Sunday		
Monday		
Tuesday		
Wednesday		
Thursday		
Friday		
Saturday		

Study Week 4: _____

Weekly Goal: This week, I will...

_____

_____

_____

_____

	Planned Time	Study Focus
Sunday		
Monday		
Tuesday		
Wednesday		
Thursday		
Friday		
Saturday		

Study Week 5: _____

Weekly Goal: This week, I will...

_____

_____

_____

_____

	Planned Time	Study Focus	
Sunday			
Monday			
Tuesday			
Wednesday			
Thursday			
Friday			
Saturday			

Study Week 6: _____

Weekly Goal: This week, I will...

_____

_____

_____

_____

	Planned Time	Study Focus
Sunday		
Monday		
Tuesday		
Wednesday		
Thursday		
Friday		
Saturday		

Study Week 7: _____

Weekly Goal: This week, I will...

_____

_____

_____

_____

	Planned Time	Study Focus	
Sunday			
Monday			
Tuesday			
Wednesday			
Thursday			
Friday			
Saturday			

Study Week 8: _____

Weekly Goal: This week, I will...

_____

_____

_____

_____

	Planned Time	Study Focus
Sunday		
Monday		
Tuesday		
Wednesday		
Thursday		
Friday		
Saturday		

Study Week 9: _____

Weekly Goal: This week, I will...

_____

_____

_____

_____

	Planned Time	Study Focus
Sunday		
Monday		
Tuesday		
Wednesday		
Thursday		
Friday		
Saturday		

Study Week 10: _____

Weekly Goal: This week, I will...

_____

_____

_____

_____

	Planned Time	Study Focus
Sunday		
Monday		
Tuesday		
Wednesday		
Thursday		
Friday		
Saturday		

Study Week 11: _____

Weekly Goal: This week, I will...

_____

_____

_____

_____

	Planned Time	Study Focus	
Sunday			
Monday			
Tuesday			
Wednesday			
Thursday			
Friday			
Saturday			

Study Week 12: _____

Weekly Goal: This week, I will...

_____

_____

_____

_____

	Planned Time	Study Focus
Sunday		
Monday		
Tuesday		
Wednesday		
Thursday		
Friday		
Saturday		

About SHRM Books

SHRM Books develops and publishes insights, ideas, strategies, and solutions on the topics that matter most to human resource professionals, people managers, and students.

The strength of our program lies in the expertise and thought leadership of our authors to educate, empower, elevate, and inspire readers around the world.

Each year, SHRM Books publishes new titles covering contemporary human resource management issues, as well as general workplace topics. With more than one hundred titles available in print, digital, and audio formats, SHRM's books can be purchased through SHRMStore.org and a variety of book retailers.

Learn more at SHRMBooks.org.

Index

Maximize your chances for success on the SHRM-CP exam.

HR professionals who prepare for SHRM certification with the SHRM Learning System consistently beat the average exam pass rate. In fact, candidates who prepare using both the SHRM BASK™ and the SHRM Learning System are 27% more likely to pass the SHRM-CP exam.

The interactive SHRM Learning System provides a customized roadmap to guide you throughout your studies.

1 A pre-test assesses your baseline knowledge and skills to help you understand your strengths and where you need to improve.

2 The portable study content is available via the online eReader or downloadable ePublications for studying offline. Printed books can be purchased if that's your preferred reading experience.

3 The interactive quizzes, flashcards, post-test, and practice exams reinforce your knowledge and build confidence for exam day.

4 A personal dashboard tracks your progress so you can quickly see completed tasks, scores, recommended next steps, and easily navigate to your next area of study.

5 More than 2,500 practice questions are built-in, including some that were previously used on actual SHRM exams.

Give yourself the best chance to succeed on the SHRM-CP exam with the SHRM Learning System. To learn more, visit **shrmcertification.org/prepare**.

SHRM®
BETTER WORKPLACES
BETTER WORLD™